Praise for *Venture Perfect*

"With icube™, we have seen an increase in sales, customers, and profits by more than 50%. The weekly meetings keep us on track and improve internal and external interaction and communication."

—Scott Lowes, Founder and CEO, Lighthouse Electronics Protection

"The rigorous icube™ process gives us clarity, helps us prioritize opportunity, and keeps us poised for success. Since icube™ is not a one-size fits all, it helps us configure the tools to best fit the size of our company and team."

—Gerry Roston, CEO, Civionics

"The principles of icube™ in *Venture Perfect* enabled us to get organized as a highly effective business development team. It has also helped us analyze marketing scientifically and scale sales in a repeatable manner."

—Cynthia Hutchison, Director of Business Development, Automation Alley

"With icube™, we now have a structure for collaboration. This gives us a shared sense of identity, which helps us make tough strategic decisions despite imperfect information. icube™ has been instrumental in helping the company attract talent and investment while keeping all stakeholders engaged."

—Brian Hayden, Founder and CEO, ShapeLog

VENTURE PERFECT

The Leadership System to Maximize
Teamwork and Profit in Your Business

Pavan V. Muzumdar

Pieris Business Press

Copyright © 2017 by Pavan Muzumdar
All rights reserved. No part of this publication may be reproduced, distributed, or transmitted in any form or by any means, including photocopying, recording, digital scanning, or other electronic or mechanical methods, without the prior written permission of the publisher, except in the case of brief quotations embodied in critical reviews and certain other noncommercial uses permitted by copyright law. For permission requests, please address:
Pieris Business Press
PO Box 7332
Bloomfield Hills, MI 48302-7332

Published 2017 by Pieris Business Press
Printed in the United States of America

20 19 18 17   1 2 3 4
ISBN 978-0-9996659-0-9
Library of Congress Control Number: 2017961432

This book is dedicated to my parents who gave so much of themselves so that my siblings and I could have everything we ever needed to enjoy a good life. They succeeded. It is also dedicated to the unbounded entrepreneurial spirit of humanity that continues to make the world a better place.

Acknowledgments

icube™ and this book are a result of what I have learned on the journey of life. I have lost count of the people who have directly or indirectly contributed to making this a reality. I would fail miserably if I were to attempt to name them all. Even so, it would be remiss of me to not mention some of them here.

As with most works of creation, there are elements of art and science. My wonderful editor and coach, Jeannie Ballew of Edit Prose, helped me conceive the book, stay on track, and communicate effectively. Our coaching sessions were always fun and engaging, and I am looking forward to doing this again soon.

A special thanks to Tom Kelly and the team at Automation Alley for believing in and embracing the icube™ principles, tools, and processes. You have been wonderful to work with and your efforts have made the company a shining example of a collaborative, learning organization.

To my partners and colleagues in all of the different companies that have made icube™ the powerful system that it is. Thanks to Joe and Lana Volpe for having the faith in me to run the companies that they had painstakingly built. Thank you to Angela Barbash, Clara Balliet, Debbie Ederer, Eric Davis, Jim Diefenbach, Marshel Barbash, and Neil Miller for being a joy to work with. To my clients in all the different companies that jumped right in and transformed their companies and teams.

Thank you to Turtlechele Media for evocative illustrations. And to the team at Thomson-Shore publications for making this book come alive with your exceptional design capabilities.

Finally, as I mention in the Introduction, this is a derivative work. It rests on the accomplishments of others before me and is primarily a packaging of powerful concepts discovered or designed by people before me. I am sure there are many more in this list that I have learned from over the years. Some of the more influential and inspirational ones include the following: Benjamin Graham, Dan Ariely, Frank Lane, Frederick Winslow Taylor, Gino Wickman, Jack Stack, James Harvey, Jim Collins, Malcolm Gladwell, Marjorie Kelly, Nicholas Taleb, Patrick Lencioni, Phil Rosenzweig, Raj Sisodia, Richard Koch, Richard Thaler, Stephen Covey, Tom Steding, Ph.D, W. Edwards Deming, and Warren Buffett.

Contents

Foreword xiii

Introduction. 1

SECTION 1: NEED A REMODEL?

1: Wiped Out! 9

    The Issues 11

    Second Stage and What it Feels Like 13

    How Companies Grow 14

2: The Diagnostic. 21

    The icube™ Diagnostic 23

    The Three "i"s 23

    Ten Statements 24

    Putting it all Together 26

    What Is the Diagnostic Looking for? 27

SECTION 2: PLANNING AND BUDGETING

3: The Elements of a Learning Organization 33

    Sources of Complexity 34

    Success: The Root Causes of Complexity 35

    How Can Your Company Grow Like Wildfire
but Manage Complexity? 37

    The Essence of Value Creation 38

    The icube™ Framework 39

    Inspiration Defined 40

    Intelligence Defined 41

    Intensity Defined 42

    Why Trust? 44

    Confidence and Arrogance 45

    Navigating Risk. 49

4: The Journey. 53

    Steps Along the icube™ Journey. 54

    What Is Covered in Steps 1-5? 55

        Steps 1 and 2: Intensity Day. 56

        Step 3: Vision Building Workshop 56

        Step 4: Positioning and Branding Workshop. 57

        Step 5: Quarterly Strategic Review Session 57

SECTION 3: DEMOLITION

5: Intensity Day 65

    Inensity Day Part 1: Morning 65

    Goals of Intensity Day 67

    Preparing for the Session. 68

    Agenda of Intensity Day. 70

        Check-in. 71

        System of Work. 71

        Team. 79

    Intensity Day Part 2: Afternoon 93

        Numbers 93

        Meeting Beats 100

        Wildly Important Goals. 102

    Issues List Review 104

    Trello Setup Plan. 106

    Closing 107

6: Weekly Tactical Meetings. 113

    The Single Most Important Factor to Ensure Success. 115

    Why Most Meetings Are Terrible 116

    The Four Stages of a Successful Meeting 119

    The Tactical Meeting Agenda 121

    How to Facilitate an Effective Tactical Meeting 122

    Dos of Great Tactical Meetings 128

    Don'ts of Great Tactical Meetings. 129

SECTION 4: CONSTRUCTION

7: Vision Building and Branding 137

    The Four Components of Inspiration 139

    Vision-Building Workshop. 139

    Positioning and Brand Strategy Workshop 147

8: Strategic Planning Beat 163

    Goals of the Strategic Meeting Beat 164

    Preparing for the Session. 165

    Agenda of the Strategic Review. .166

    Break Down of the Strategic Review Agenda. 166

SECTION 5: CLEAN UP

9: Objections, Costs, and Risks of Using icube™. 179

    Objections to Using icube™. 181

    Cost and Self-Facilitation. 186

    Three Ways to Facilitate icube™ 187

    Risks of Facilitating icube™ 189

    Pros and Cons of Using Trello 190

10: Beyond icube™ 193

    Departmental Tactical and Strategic Meetings
Beyond the Leadership Team 195

    Advanced Scorecard Concepts and Gainsharing 200

    Establishment of a Functioning Board 201

    Effective Use of Information Systems 202

    Company Growth Dynamics 203

    Critical icube™ Concepts in a Nutshell 205

Appendix: Robert and Meetings 209

References 215

Figures

    1.1 The Boss is the Bottleneck 15

    1.2 Stages of the Entrepreneur 17

    2.1 The Three "i"s 23

    3.1 Sources of Complexity 35

    3.2 The Essence of Value Creation 38

    3.3a Inspiration 40

    3.3b Intelligence 41

    3.3c Intensity 43

    3.4 The icube™ Framework 44

    3.5 Why Trust? 45

    3.6 Confidence and Arrogance 46

    3.7 Navigating Risk 50

    4.1 Steps in the icube™ Journey 55

    5.1 The Cycle of Execution 73

5.2   The Flow of Work 74

5.3   The icube™ Functional Framework 81

5.4   Johari Window Blindspots. 90

5.5   Number Categories 94

5.6   Categorizing Issues 105

5.7   Light Craft Innovations' Functional Framework . . . 108

6.1   The Four Stages of a Successful Meeting. 119

6.2   Light Craft Innovations' Tactical Trello Meeting Board .127

7.1   The Universal Brand Challenge 150

8.1   Sample Inspiration Board. 169

9.1   The Universal Brand Challenge 182

10.1   Tactical Meeting Groupings .196

10.2   How Companies Grow. 203

Tables

2.1   Light Craft Innovations' icube™ Diagnostic 27

5.1   System of Work Audit 78

5.2   Examples of Measures 99

5.3   Scorecard Worksheet 99

5.4   Scorecard for Light Craft Innovations, LLC. 109

Foreword

As CEO of Automation Alley, Michigan's leading nonprofit technology and manufacturing membership-based business association, I have the privilege of working with Pavan Muzumdar as our Chief Operating Officer and lead facilitator of icube™. Our mission is to position Southeast Michigan as a global leader in Industry 4.0, the fourth industrial revolution in which digital technologies such as cloud computing and artificial intelligence combine with physical technologies like robotics and 3D printing. These technologies are causing exponential changes in traditional fields such as manufacturing. We help our members increase revenue, reduce costs, and think strategically as they keep pace with such rapid technological changes in manufacturing. In order to fuel Southeast Michigan's economy and accelerate innovation, we connect our members with industry, academia, and government. Automation Alley focuses its efforts on innovation and technology, entrepreneurship, talent development, defense, and international business. We provide resources, funding, and actionable intelligence to help members grow and prosper in the digital age.

Back in 2014, I became the director of entrepreneurship at Automation Alley. I was new to the role and was given carte blanche to shake the program down to the studs and rebuild. Funded through the Michigan Economic Development Corporation (MEDC), I developed a program we eventually called the 7Cs. The 7Cs program was designed from the ground up to apply knowledge and resources in the proper dosage and at the proper time to allow a business to grow quickly, and most important, independently of outside investment other than sales. To accomplish that objective, I was convinced that the cornerstone of the 7Cs program had to be change management consulting. I arrived at this conclusion from my years of technology start-up consulting at the Michigan Small Business Technology Development Center (MI-SBTDC). I advised over 300 clients and found that there was always a consistent theme. The start-ups' technology was rarely the problem; the teams invariably lacked the ability to manage rapid change across many functional lines such as sales, marketing, operations, and finance. I was determined to solve this persistent yet common problem through our new 7Cs program, so I looked at quite a few programs, and through sheer luck and good timing happened to run into an old acquaintance, Pavan. As he explained his icube™ system to me, I became convinced that icube™ could be a game-changer for our 7Cs clients. We agreed to roll out the system with our first, new 7Cs' client, Lighthouse Electronics Protection (LEP). As we geared up to launch icube™ with LEP, I also decided that we should "eat our own dogfood" in industry parlance, so we started using the icube™ system within the small entrepreneurial department of Automation Alley. A year later, upon my promotion to Chief Operating Officer, we rolled out icube™ company wide. In keeping with icube™'s philosophy of the dual leadership roles of Promoter and Conductor, when I moved into the CEO position (Promoter), we hired Pavan as our COO (Conductor). We haven't looked back since.

We have been using the icube™ system for several years now, and the transformation of the organization has been nothing short of extraordinary. Automation Alley is a relatively complex business in relation to its size as we have initiatives in foreign direct investment, exporting and trade missions, entrepreneurship, manufacturing, defense, talent retention and upskilling, and membership services. Getting everyone to understand a common mission, purpose, and vision and to "row in the same direction" has always been a challenge for us, but the icube™ system has made a remarkable difference. icube™ helps you define what is important and forces you to confront and solve problems in a systematic way that holds all employees accountable and drives results. This accountability is the cornerstone of the icube™ system as it builds trust through transparency and common purpose without micro-managing people. It allows people to do their best work and be recognized instantly and automatically for "moving the needle." Through icube™, we defined one culture with one purpose. This led to deeper and more insightful questions about our markets, customers, and initiatives, which, in turn, inspired more effective execution. The speed and intensity of execution is the payoff for us as we have increased sales while reducing costs, and now see the business through a strategic lens that has made all the difference. An example of this ability to rapidly execute new initiatives is our brand-new Tech Takeover Series initiative.

It was conceived and introduced in 2017 as a program comprised of ninety-six events during a calendar year to provide high-quality content to manufacturing companies. The laser focus facilitated by icube™ enabled us to make this a resounding success. All Tech Takeover slots have been filled for the rest of the year. Considering that Automation Alley is a non-profit, this program is generating enough new revenues to provide the organization with additional resources to execute our mission. Similarly, our ability to drive results in our other initiatives is enabling Automation Alley to be recognized as the Michigan Center for Industry 4.0.

The most important difference icube™ has made to our organization is transparent accountability, which builds trust, forces competence, and helps us drive results. In addition, our team members consistently report feeling more engaged and satisfied because they are part of an important purpose greater than themselves, which also helps them find more meaning in their work. I could not be more pleased with our success using icube™ and wholeheartedly endorse the systems and methods employed within it. It has made a transformative difference to Automation Alley, and I suspect, if you can relate to Diana in the story, it will make a remarkable difference to you and your organization, as well.

Thomas Kelly
CEO and Executive Director
Automation Alley

Introduction

"Well, Jackie, you wouldn't have all these problems if you hadn't built a multi-million-dollar business."

What if the path to profit and prosperity in a business wasn't so difficult? What if all employees were to reap direct financial rewards when their companies are successful and profitable? What if employees were so deeply invested in the outcome of their work and felt empowered to make changes and contributions that they couldn't be distinguished from the owners? At the risk of sounding grandiose, the information I'm about to share has the potential to ignite prosperity and solve the problems of financial inequity in any capitalistic democratic society. After reading this book, if I have done my job as a writer, it is my sincere hope that you will never look at business the same way ever again.

I was born in India, and even though I arrived on the threshold of adulthood, I "grew up" in America. It was like a reset button was pushed, and my vantage point suddenly shifted. That realization only became apparent, however, after I reflected on my journey in one of the rest stops of my career. My professional journey has been anything but linear. It reminds me of the Stanford commencement address by Steve Jobs in which he talks about connecting the dots. Who knew that it would take so much time for it to finally make sense?

I started my career as a software developer for an innovative systems integration firm during the early 1990s, serving Fortune 500 companies. From there, I moved to the Midwest and was firmly ensconced in small business America, leading a software company.

Along the way I was tasked with overseeing a couple of mid-market companies that, despite being successful in their respective markets, were performing far below their potential. The same issues and lack of alignment in the team came up time and again. Even though I was able to come up with operational solutions, we just couldn't find a way to make them stick. Frankly, the leadership team and I were in over our heads and weren't sure how to handle the growing complexity of the organization.

This created a deep desire in me to find out why some companies succeed whereas others fail. Becoming proficient in financial analysis by securing the CFA charter unveiled for me the elements of successful organizations. Eventually, as I understood what success looked like, I started delving into understanding the factors that led to success. Once I began to understand complex issues, I learned why my earlier solutions weren't working. The simple fact was that there was very little trust in the organizations, and no matter how good the solutions were, they wouldn't be accepted and implemented until trust was established. I realized that in order to build trust, leaders had to understand and influence the core of the culture (Inspiration), so that it could guide the strategy (Intelligence), which could then lead to excellent execution (Intensity). This insight is what gave birth to PCS Insight and the icube™ system. Inspiration, Intelligence and Intensity are the three "i"s in icube™.

It also became clear to me that trust, ownership, and team member engagement are intertwined. When people feel like they are owners, they care and have high levels of engagement in the work they do. When others see their teammates displaying high levels of engagement, they trust them and in turn feel more engaged and feel a higher sense of ownership in their work and toward the organization. This cycle of engagement, ownership, and trust is the foundation of effective organizations and at the core of every strong culture. It is something we must foster in organizations moving forward. As the following paragraphs describe, not doing so may very well undermine our system of government and way of life.

Starting with the industrial age, there has always been tension between technology and manual labor. The ability to make our lives easier often comes at a price to others. Some people benefit with cheaper, better, faster, and more useful tools while others lose their jobs. The difference, however, is that for the first time, modern technological advances such as artificial intelligence are striking at the core of human cognition. What used to be a "blue-collar" problem has seeped into "white-collar" professions.

Many people are fearful of these new advancements in automated technologies and smart robotics because they may one day make many human jobs obsolete, resulting in increased poverty and wealth disparity. These are the same fears that existed with previous industrial revolutions. Think about the invention of the printing press or even the telephone.

As people become disgruntled over potential job loss, tensions rise between the class of "owners" and "employees." History has shown time and again that this is how revolutions start – the disenfranchised with less to lose seek to take power back from those who control the wealth. If we are to avoid the next revolution, our mindset needs to shift from "us vs. them" to a collective "we." This doesn't mean overhauling our economy to a communist or socialist system. Instead, we need to transform our current capitalist system into "conscious capitalism," one in which those who seek more wealth can do so, but not at the expense of others. Instead, there can be an opportunity to change the world as we know it for the better.

How is this accomplished? Right now, owners believe they take all the risk, so they believe they deserve all the reward. Though owners tend to think like this, it's important to realize that while all owners have risk, they don't share it equally. But changing this mindset is the key to unlocking the potential of a more advanced society. What if everyone thought and behaved as an owner? And what if every employee were rewarded like an owner for their contributions?

To be sure, when we ask these questions, we are also changing the paradigm of what it means to be an owner. In fact, we can distinguish between looking at ownership as a claim versus ownership as a state of mind, a feeling of responsibility. In my worldview, ownership doesn't just mean a claim to assets; instead, it is a responsibility to nurture those assets for the greater good. If you are an employee who has an ownership mindset, one might argue that there is little reward for taking responsibility to nurture the assets for the greater good, aside from a feeling of satisfaction, if there is no monetary reward. But in the system I am presenting, one can have both: profit and greater good. Many people who identify as employees today do not feel like owners, and that's understandable. Companies are not usually designed with this intent in mind, and leaders often do not have the tools at their disposal to foster an ownership mindset.

That's the one thing I hope to change with this book. With icube™, leaders of growing companies can learn how to increase profits by intensifying happiness in the workplace. We do this by helping all employees think like owners. To know what an ownership mindset feels like, think about your most prized possession. If you're a business owner, it might very well be your business. If you're not, perhaps it's something else such as your house, your car, or perhaps even a beloved pet. Now think about what you would do if something affected your business, the car broke down, the house needed repairs, or your pet wasn't feeling well. You would rush to fix the problem with care and attention often without concern for yourself in the moment. That's the ownership mindset.

When everyone in a business cares for it like an owner, it reduces human friction by ensuring that all team members have the same intentions. This results in greater productivity and long-term success. If you think this is pie-in-the-sky, not so fast! There are many examples of this in the real world. For example, the John Lewis Partnership in the UK (https://www.johnlewispartnership.co.uk/) and SRC Holdings Corporation, Springfield, MO (http://srcholdings.com/), to name a few, are practicing the very concepts taught in this book. In my home state of Michigan, the Zingerman's Community of Businesses (http://www.zingermanscommunity.com) is also a wonderful example. These companies have a strong tradition of employee equity ownership complemented by employee training to foster the ownership mindset described earlier. The SRC Holdings story is described in the book, *The Great Game of Business,* by Jack Stack, and you can read more about The John Lewis Partnership and other examples of companies that exemplify the ownership mindset in the book,

Owning Our Future, by Marjorie Kelly. The Zingerman's story can be found at the following link: https://www.zingermanscommunity.com/about-us/a-bit-of-zingermans-history/. I would encourage you to read more about how these are structured, how they benefit employees, and how they continue to generate high profits.

If everyone working in a company had literal (financial compensation) and figurative (ownership mindset) ownership in it, then all interests would be aligned, and the ultimate objective of owners would be to make companies as prosperous as possible. While sharing the equity in a business is one way of sharing ownership, it's not the only way to do so. For example, some companies share non-voting stock that can receive dividends but may not directly impact decision making. Other companies implement gainsharing systems that foster a collaborative team environment. The most important factor is that the solution reinforces the behavior and ownership mindset by having the transparency and incentives in place.

When all interests are aligned, the collective ownership is more likely to embrace any technology that helps productivity to skyrocket. In the past, productivity improvements were incremental and still needed human input. Some of the productivity improvements that we are seeing today, however, have built into them artificial intelligence resembling human cognition. We are seeing technology that enables cars to drive themselves, software to analyze x-rays to diagnose diseases, and advanced robots that can perform many tasks that used to take a skilled human operator.

The direct impact of all this automation in the workplace is a boost in productivity and a reduction in human labor. When there is broad-based ownership, the benefits of this productivity are distributed to all owners in the form of increased dividends, potentially compensating for any lost earnings due to decreasing wages because of jobs lost to automation. In fact, we now have the opportunity for robots and humans to work more closely. Collaboration is the key to accelerating prosperity. Instead of fearing automation, we can use our brains for higher level thinking, thereby increasing our potential to solve the world's greatest mysteries while our robot partners do the mundane, dangerous, mind-numbing tasks.

The other big opportunity we have reveals itself when we look at the needs of humans and robots. Robots just need energy. When we get up in the morning, we're reminded that we have all the energy we need from the sun. The more sustainable energy we harvest, the easier it will be for robots to become self-sufficient. We can build robots that build robots that make solar panels!

As technology advances, energy from higher density solar areas can be transferred to less sunny areas. That energy can be used to fill one of our other needs: food. Also, cheaper energy means cheaper shelter. And more advanced sustainable methods for sourcing water become economically viable.

Humans, on the other hand, need food, water and shelter to survive. But we are also social, thoughtful, and curious creatures who crave knowledge and meaning. The psychologist Abraham Maslow artfully described this in his seminal work, *The Hierarchy of Human Needs.* After basic needs such as food, clothing, shelter and security are met, humans need social connections, self-esteem, and fulfillment of their purpose, in that order. With the help of our robot friends, maybe we can all elevate ourselves up this hierarchy. In this vision, education and learning are the ends and means of a fruitful and joyous journey, all while working for highly successful companies that we love and help to build.

SECTION 1: NEED A REMODEL?

"It is not the strongest or the most intelligent who will survive, but those who can best manage change."

—Charles Darwin

1: Wiped Out!

"Mom, aren't sports supposed to be fun?"

Light Craft in the Spotlight

Diana slumped back in her chair with a sigh. She had just gotten off the phone with Angela Seyler, the President of Global Organization of Lighting Designers (GOLD) who had asked her to chair the standards committee for the organization in recognition of her creativity and innovation in the industry. She thanked the president profusely and promised to get back with a reply within a few weeks. A prestigious position by any measure, just a few years ago this would have been Diana's dream call. But now, she hated calls like this.

Light Craft is a designer of high-end, custom, indoor and outdoor lighting design solutions. They work primarily with architects and general contractors in the commercial real estate development space. Light Craft has won many awards for its unique designs and has an excellent reputation for being a thought leader in this specialized industry. So why would the owner of a successful, well regarded company not want to be recognized for her contributions? To find out, let's go back in time.

Light Craft Innovations, Inc. was founded by Diana and her business partner at the time, Michael LeClerc. When they first started, Diana and Michael decided that they would start the business as equals. Diana was not only a designer, but she also had a knack for business development and was the clear leader of the company. Michael, on the other hand, was much happier in front of a design workstation. A year and a half later, however, Michael realized that while lighting design was interesting, his heart was in designing high-end custom furniture. Wood, not light, was this artist's medium of choice.

A few years ago, an architect client of Light Craft approached the company about a different kind of a lighting design project. It was a mansion for Bobby Fields, the tech billionaire. Bobby was known to be a patron of the arts and one to appreciate real talent. Michael was the lead designer on the project. Through a series of conversations, Bobby found out about Michael's talents and passion for wood working and in typical Fields's fashion made him an offer he couldn't refuse: Michael could have the opportunity to create a one-of-a-kind boutique custom furniture business. Bobby would bring in the business and enough affluent friends to keep Michael busy for two lifetimes. Michael was ecstatic, and Diana knew better than to stand in his way. They shook hands, hugged, and just like that, after executing a simple purchase agreement, with a cocktail of nervousness and excitement flowing through her veins, Diana became a 100% owner of Light Craft.

Firmly in the driver's seat, Diana unleashed her energies, and Light Craft blossomed into an industry leader in commercial lighting design. From a team of four people, including herself and Michael, Light Craft grew to thirty people on staff with revenues just over $10.5 million and a robust profit margin.

Over the last couple of years, Light Craft had found itself using LED lighting in most of its projects. While there was a lot of interest in LED lighting, the technology was so new that the industry was creating best practices on the fly. With little developed in the way of standards, Light Craft found itself becoming a leader in creating them, also on the fly. The industry had taken notice, and Diana was being asked to speak at industry events, most recently at GOLD's international congress, to present some of Light Craft's groundbreaking work.

Diana enjoyed the exposure and also saw the value in it because of the leads it generated, but she also found herself overwhelmed at times because when she left the office to attend industry events, she came back to a mountain of paperwork and tasks not finished to her satisfaction. Not to mention that she was finding herself increasingly irritated with people in the company for not being able to take care of things. And that brings us to the conversation she just had with Ms. Seyler, president of GOLD.

Diana opened her email inbox and from the corner of her eye she could see the red flashing "voicemail" indicator on the phone. There were fifty-three "urgent" unread email messages. They didn't include any of the lower priority messages such as subscriptions and unsolicited messages that she received in the hundreds. These required her immediate attention. Most of the messages were from her office manager, Jackie Davis, about various accounting, billing, and purchasing questions. Others were from Raj Patel, Light Craft's senior designer, who was requesting clarification on design issues and a meeting with him and other team members, including Mike Burns, project specialist, and Theresa Janovic, assistant designer. They had a disagreement and needed Diana's input to resolve it. The rest of the emails were from other members of her team, clients, and vendors and covered a smattering of issues for her to hear, comment, decide, suggest, bless, arbitrate, referee, mediate, analyze, guide, or resolve!

None of these items were super critical by themselves, but they all needed attention *now*. And today was just a repeat of yesterday, which was a repeat of the day before. With all of this on her plate, Diana couldn't see the joy of serving on the standards committee. Not one to be easily overwhelmed, she felt stuck, repeating the same day over and over like in the movie *Groundhog Day*.

How can I keep this company going and do a good job on the committee? she thought. She plowed through the emails and voicemails, and by the time she was done, it was late. She slowly picked up her car keys and headed out the door like a zombie, completely wiped out.

The Issues

That weekend Diana decided that she would try to figure out what was happening. She drove to her favorite coffee shop and settled into a quiet corner close to a window. The café was near a college, and it appeared that the students had other things on their minds than sitting indoors, sipping lattes. Diana appreciated the calm, pulled out her notepad and started listing everything about the business that was bothering her. Her stream of consciousness produced the following bulleted list:

- Poor collaboration between team members. Then I have to get involved in mundane issues and that is a waste of my time.
- Team members not understanding the business. I feel like I explain the same thing over and over. This is a total waste of my time!
- Team members not feeling like their work has meaning or that they are a part of something worthwhile. This is so disheartening. I don't know how to inspire them.
- Ineffective meetings in which team members regrind the same tired issues over and over. It's exhausting. And then I have to put my foot down to make things happen, and I end up feeling like the corporate witch. And I resent it!
- Virtually no independent problem solving, forward momentum or follow through. I am sick of handholding. Why can't these people take some initiative?
- Lack of clear process to attract customers. Business is feast or famine, resulting in growth appearing in fits and starts.
- Overly dependent sales team. I have to be involved in every little aspect of the sales process, however minute, or nothing gets done.
- Inefficient systems. I have a nagging feeling that things could be done better.
- Unclear definition of roles and responsibilities. There is a lot of finger pointing when things go wrong.

After Diana privately ranted about her team, a little voice inside wondered how much of this was her own doing. She recalled the time recently when she had brought a promising designer on board, and he had asked her an innocent question. Diana's irritation and her biting response surprised him. She later realized that it was uncalled for and apologized. The damage, however, was done, and he soon left to work for another firm.

That's just not like me she thought. *I have never been one to bite someone's head off if they asked a rookie question. Heck, I would have asked something like that myself twenty years ago. Maybe it's time to do something else.*

Second Stage and What it Feels Like

As much as Diana thought her situation was unique, this happens time and again in companies. According to many experts who have studied the growth of companies, Diana's company is in "second stage." An expert in second stage company dynamics, Dino Signore, manager of entrepreneurial education at The Edward Lowe Foundation in Cassopolis, Michigan, describes it this way in his article titled, "Second-Stage Sensei."

> On the plus side, second-stagers have a proven product or service under their belts and have attracted initial customers, so survival is no longer a daily concern. Yet as they strive to gain a stronger foothold in the market and win more customers, second-stagers now face more strategic issues, such as building infrastructure to scale, honing their competitive edge and expanding into new markets.

I thought the best way to describe how it feels to be a second stage entrepreneur would be to borrow from stand-up comic Jeff Foxworthy's, "You might be a redneck" routine. So with apologies and deference to Mr. Foxworthy, here goes:

You might be a second-stage entrepreneur if . . .

- ◇ You have a team, but you're the first one in and the last to leave.
- ◇ You would describe yourself as too big to be small but too small to be big.
- ◇ You're making money, but you don't quite know how to say what you do.
- ◇ You're not eating Ramen noodles anymore, but there's no time for a steak dinner.
- ◇ You're finding that how got you here isn't quite getting you where you want to go.

- ◇ You want to be the quarterback, but really you need to be the coach.
- ◇ You're not the chief bottle-washer anymore, but you're not sure if the bottles are getting washed.

How Companies Grow

To understand why it feels this way in second stage, let's look at how companies grow naturally.

Stage 1

Most companies start with a founder who has the passion and drive to do something on his or her own. These business owners often have special skills they use to provide a product or service for which they see a need in the marketplace. With an added dose of grit and hard work, they are able to generate some repeat business. In this stage, the founder manages the Sales and the Operations in the business.

> *Stage 1.1*
>
> As the business continues, the owner adds more people to the team and separates Sales and Operations. Most of the time, they do this by hiring additional employees. More often than not, the owner realizes that he or she can provide some level of training to these new members so that they can do the work of delivering the product or service, i.e., handle Operations, while the founder is responsible for generating the Sales.

> *Stage 1.5*
>
> Along the way, the owner recognizes the need to manage money and the accounting responsibilities in the business, which by now has started developing some financial complexity in the form of tracking receivables and payables, tax obligations, and expenses of some magnitude. An accounting person, usually a bookkeeper, is added to the mix, and since the business owner is firmly in charge, the lines of reporting are directly between the bookkeeper and the owner.

Stage 2

Stage 1.5 continues and slowly morphs into Stage 2. Somewhere along the way, the owner adds some marketing to the company in the form of a website facelift. Initially, it is often a DIY effort or put together by a web designer who doesn't really understand the business. The website is usually a reflection of the owner's ideas and rarely has input from the rest of the team. The company also develops collateral in the form of brochures, flyers, and anything else to generate exposure for the company that is appropriate for its industry. At this point, the business is usually on firm footing and making money, however, something is not quite right. The owner is in the middle of everything and nothing at the same time. Sometimes he or she feels like the team, including other leaders, are on a different planet, doing their own thing or like they can't do anything without any direction. This happens because the original organizational structure of the company was one boss who rules over the company, but this is unsustainable as the company grows. Typically, the boss elevates the Accounting function to serve as a buffer between Sales and Operations but continues to influence them independently, often without communicating this to the Accounting personnel. And Marketing ends up being a separate function, usually filled by an outside company, reporting solely to the boss with no communication with the rest of the organization. The boss becomes the bottleneck and the structure ends up looking like the organization chart shown in Figure 1.1.

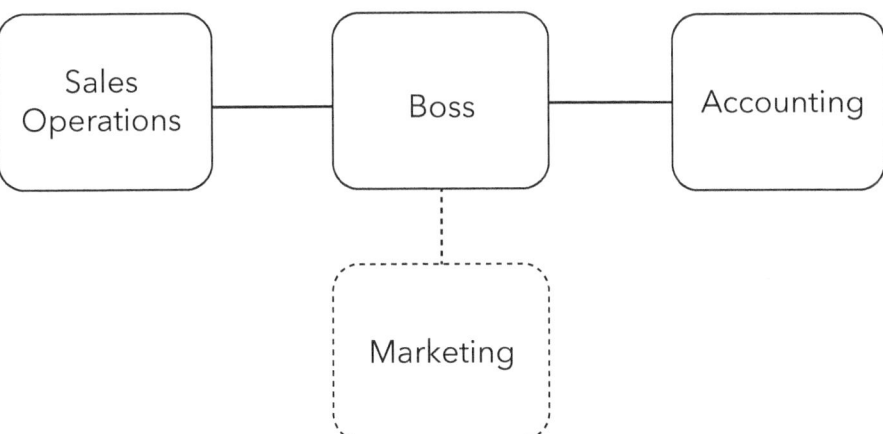

Figure 1.1: The Boss is the Bottleneck

To be sure, this organizational structure can be very effective, and in industries that don't change much, a company can even thrive. All functions are focused on execution, and if there are no changes in the external environment, they can help the company generate profit for long periods. Some bosses who are at the center of these kinds of structures even like it and want to keep it that way because the daily fires and activities give them a sense of control and the attention they like.

The problems, however, with this kind of structure are two-fold: 1) A company that runs like this will find it very hard to learn and adapt. Marketing, which is the external facing function in most companies, needs to have access to the "on the street" knowledge that Sales and Operations functions have. Accounting needs to be aware of all of the goings on in the business to be able to help the company make money related decisions more intelligently; and 2) More important, as we can see from the figure, this kind of an organizational structure requires the boss to be in at all times. The company becomes a personality lead organization as opposed to team lead. Not only does this make the presence of the boss critical, but it can lead to burnout and frustration. This was what Diana, the owner of Light Craft, was experiencing.

A visual representation of this experience is in Figure 1.2. Stage 1 and 1.1 encompass the first third of the graphic. In the early stage, the founder spends time creating and leading. This is fun and energizing. As the company becomes more successful, the founder finds his or her efforts increasingly taken up by technical work. Life is still somewhat enjoyable because the work is relevant to the passion of the entrepreneur and fruits of labor are apparent even though the time spent creating and leading is somewhat minimized.

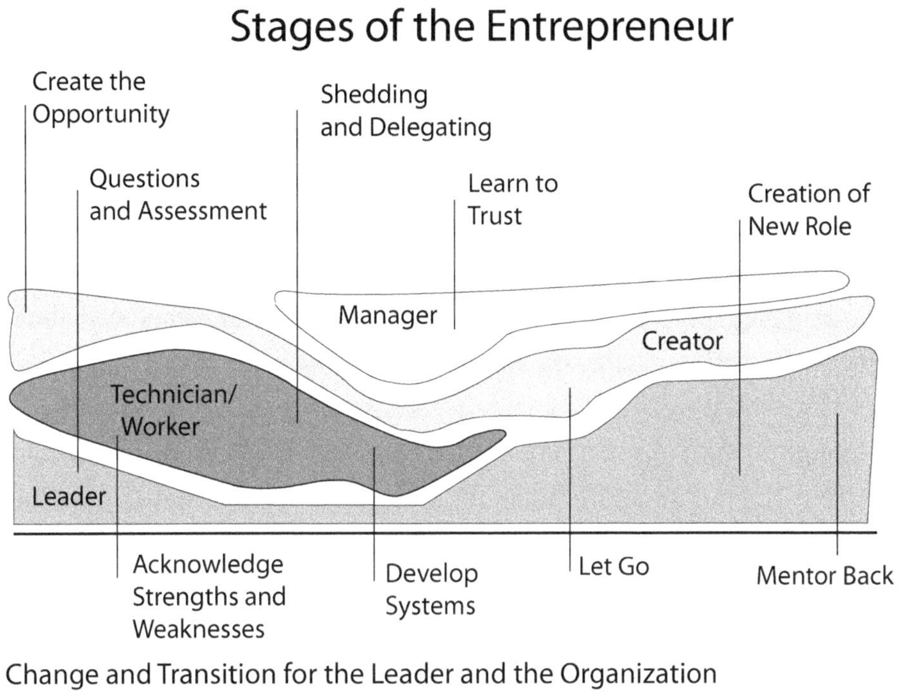
Stages of the Entrepreneur
Create the Opportunity
Shedding and Delegating
Questions and Assessment
Learn to Trust
Creation of New Role
Manager
Creator
Technician/ Worker
Leader
Acknowledge Strengths and Weaknesses
Develop Systems
Let Go
Mentor Back
Change and Transition for the Leader and the Organization

Figure 1.2: Stages of the Entrepreneur
(reproduced with permission from the Edward Lowe Foundation)

As the company grows, however, into the middle or second third of the graphic, more of the entrepreneur's time is spent managing with less time for creation, technical work, and leading. This is the height of second stage and where Diana is currently. Most founders don't really enjoy managing, but in the absence of an alternative, they find themselves having to do it, and that's when they get frustrated and irritated. Some companies and founders stay in this stage for long periods of time and may even stay that way till they burn out or decide to sell their companies.

Another outcome of this is that we end up with the owner of the company on one side and the employees on the other. The frustration that ensues is like a cloud that hangs over the business, and while everybody feels it, it's difficult to articulate, resulting in a general feeling of employees thinking that they need to show up for work because *they have to.* Unfortunately, many companies run like this, and it is the primary reason I wrote this book. It doesn't have to be this way. When all team members are engaged in a business and think like owners, profit and productivity shoot up.

Imagine what it would be like if you had a company in which everybody felt like his or her favorite part of the week was Sunday night. And imagine how it would feel if the thought of going to work energized you, the prospect of having a team meeting was exciting, and every Friday afternoon you basked in the glow of contentment from having accomplished everything you set out to do. Imagine a company in which the marketing system was generating plenty of leads, the sales team was kicking out orders, the company had emails and calls from customers describing the delight they experienced, and finally there was plenty of profit to compensate everybody handsomely, invest in the future of the business, and save for a rainy day. Sounds like a pipe dream? Not at all. You can do this in your company if you follow the principles described in this book. Along the way you will have an engaged work force that loves their work and a company that is built to last.

I strongly urge you to go back and read the Introduction to learn why I think that businesses no longer have to settle for the status quo. In fact, not settling is essential for the future of our system of government and our prosperity.

A company that breaks through second stage provides a refreshing and energizing experience for a founder and the team. By building the organizational structure, the System of Work, and measurement tools, the founder is able to let go and spend less time on managing and more time on leading and creating. This is his or her natural state and is really why he or she started his or her company in the first place. Along the way, the rest of the team starts feeling they are also owners of the business, and the work is no longer a chore. Instead, it has meaning and purpose and can even be joy filled. Diana needed to get to this place, and intuitively she knew that a chat with Robert, her business mentor, would help get her there.

Coffee Talk with Robert

Diana first met Robert a few years ago at a local chamber of commerce event. They served on a committee together and had the opportunity to work together. She noticed that he had an easygoing manner along with the ability to cut through seemingly intractable challenges and get to the core issue very quickly. She also noticed that he was comfortable with his success and didn't need to hog the limelight. As the elder statesman, he would encourage the younger leaders in the group, including Diana, to take calculated risks and give them opportunities for growth and recognition in the community. Over time, he became Diana's friend and business mentor, and they often got together with their respective families.

Robert started A2Z Distributing in the late 70s primarily focusing on being an aftermarket supplier of specialized automotive components. With blood, sweat, and tears, he built a successful company that dominated the niche in which it operated. Robert ensured that A2Z's focus on excellent service made it a no brainer for its customers to do business with it. Manufacturers took notice and offered A2Z coveted master distributor status with attractive credit terms. Robert took the opportunity, added to his team, and over time, A2Z became a well-known brand in the automotive services community. (See Appendix to learn how a crisis moved Robert and his team to implement icube™. Robert's story also raises the issue of how to run effective meetings. This will be fully fleshed out in Chapter 6.)

Robert was happy to get Diana's voicemail and request to get together for coffee, and they decided to meet at their regular haunt. "So, how are Eric and the kids?" Robert opened with a smile.

"As wonderful as ever! Eric's doing very well in his work at the institute, and the kids are enjoying school," Diana beamed. "And how's Julie?"

"Great! She's teaching me the basics of quantum mechanics. Very interesting stuff if you ask me," he replied. Robert's wife Julie was a physics professor at the local university. "You know, I'm a guy who's very comfortable with machines, moving parts, and stuff you can touch and feel. But this microscopic, nano-scale world is fascinating and counter-intuitive. It's opened my eyes. My simple way of interpreting quantum mechanics, which, by the way, can really get your mind in a loop, is that it's best to keep an open mind. What I once thought to be certain, no longer is. What I once thought I completely understood isn't quite what I thought it was. The learning continues!"

"Sounds very interesting and a great segue for why I called you to meet for coffee. Robert, I thought I loved being in business for myself, but now I'm not so sure." Diana described her feelings to Robert and showed him her list of issues. She illustrated her point by showing him her calendar for the past week. At one point, she even said that she was wavering in her confidence as leader of Light Craft. But when she was done, she was surprised to see that far from being alarmed or showing any concern, Robert was smiling.

"I've waited many years to say this to you Diana. Welcome to second stage!" he proclaimed.

"Second who?" asked Diana with a frown.

"Second stage. It's when a company is past survival, ready to grow, and also when the founder is sometimes ready to call it quits. Happens more often than not, and A2Z went through it also just a few years before we met. In fact, had we met each other while A2Z was in that phase, you would most likely have found me to be insufferable, impatient, and irritable. Fortunately, we found a way out. We implemented icube™, and it's the best thing we have ever done for the company. It may be something Light Craft is also ready for, and there's a simple way to find out."

We'll pick up Diana's story again in Chapter 2, but for now, let's review some housekeeping notes. As described in the Introduction, there are two ways to read this book. The first approach, which I call the "Vision Track," is to take a high-level view of the concepts. The second is the "Action Track," which is to actually implement them in your team or company. At the end of each chapter, we will pause and ask the relevant questions pertaining to each track.

One final note: the two tracks are not mutually exclusive. My own sense is that if you want to take a first pass at it and aren't sure if icube™ is a fit for your organization, just do the Vision Track. If, on the other hand, you have already heard of icube™ and are ready to implement it, do both the Vision and the Action Tracks. Either way, I hope you find this journey exhilarating and transformational!

Vision Track

- How are you feeling right now?
- Do you feel like you are a second-stage entrepreneur?
- How many of the "You might be…" bullet points fit you?

Action Track To-Dos

- Take the afternoon off and list out all the issues or challenges that you are facing in the company.
- Prioritize the list, putting the challenges that are the most important at the top.

In the next chapter, we will dig a little deeper into issues and use a simple diagnostic tool to get to the bottom of what's causing them.

2: The Diagnostic

"Bob, in order for me to tell you how to get there,
you need to tell me where you are!"

Light Craft in the Spotlight

Back in the office the next day, Diana reviewed an email from Robert titled, *icube™ Diagnostic*. Following the title was a list of ten statements. Each statement was followed by a string of numbers from 1–10 and the words "Strongly Agree," "Strongly Disagree," and "Don't know." Robert had mentioned to her that each member of the team needs to answer the questions on their own separately and turn in their sheets to a designated compiler who enters the scores on the *icube™ Diagnostic Analyzer* spreadsheet.

When Diana looked at this tool, she was both intrigued and surprised. Before her meeting with Robert, she would never have thought that the source of her issues could be addressed by a set of ten simple statements. *This is the same thing that Robert used for his company, and A2Z is bigger and more complex than Light Craft.* She decided to take the plunge and called a team meeting.

With the entire team assembled, Diana distributed the questionnaire and asked each of them to answer the questions to the best of their ability and turn in their responses to Jackie. After a couple of days, Jackie completed the diagnostic spreadsheet. She entered each person's name in a new row and recorded their scores in the columns. Each "Don't know" was scored as a zero. She emailed the results to Diana when she was done. Diana opened the spreadsheet and immediately noticed some patterns, but she also had many questions. She sent Robert a note requesting another meeting. Before we explore the diagnostic tool, take a moment to reflect on your action steps from the previous chapter.

Build Status Check-in

Vision Track

- ◇ How are you feeling now that you've taken some of the actions suggested in the previous chapter?
- ◇ Did your reflection raise additional questions or bring about more clarity?
- ◇ Are there any issues that you would like to add to your own issues list?

Action Track

- ◇ Have you completed all the to-dos from the previous chapter?
- ◇ Are there any issues that you need to address?
- ◇ What roadblocks did you encounter?
- ◇ If you didn't finish it, what needs to happen in order for you to complete it?

The icube™ Diagnostic

We will pick up with Light Craft again later, but for now, let's dive into the *icube™ Diagnostic*. The *icube™ Diagnostic* is a simple tool designed to quickly hone in on the issues any team is facing. There are ten statements, and the objective is for every team member to evaluate each statement. Just as a tool like the Myers-Briggs Type Indicator ® helps individuals become aware of their personality preference, the *icube™ Diagnostic* helps teams uncover the sources of internal conflict and performance issues.

The Three "i"s

The core concept of icube™ is that there are three "i"s that the leaders of any organization need to develop and strengthen: 1) Inspiration, 2) Intelligence, and 3) Intensity. We'll come back to this concept in much more detail in the next chapter, but for now, here's a short introduction. Refer to Figure 2.1 to follow along.

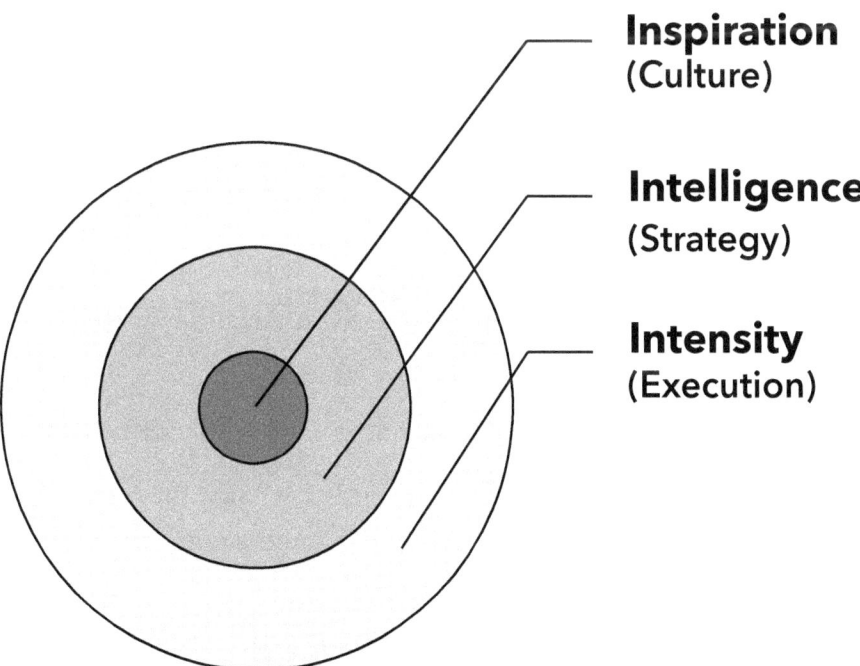

Figure 2.1: The Three "i"s

The first thing we are able to observe about a team is how it functions. In sports, this is how well the team plays the game. In business, it's how well a company attracts and retains customers, delivers products or services, and manages its resources and money. We call this Intensity. Intensity captures the ability of the team to execute.

But excellent execution, or strong Intensity, doesn't happen automatically. It's the consequence of excellent and effective planning. In sports, this is the playbook the team uses to play the game. In business, it's the strategy the leadership team develops to approach the market, satisfy customers, and generate a profit. We call strategy the Intelligence of the organization.

Finally, an effective strategy cannot be developed unless there is common purpose and a strong culture. In sports, this is reflected by the respect and coordination the team members demonstrate while playing the game. In excellent teams, you will notice that the team members can count on each other. It's pretty much the same in business. Team members must be able to count on each other in order for the company to deliver value as a whole. We call the culture and its effectiveness characterized by the level of trust in the organization the Inspiration.

The three "i"s together, Inspiration, Intelligence, and Intensity, make up the essential elements of any successful organization. If any one of them is weak, the organization as a whole will be weak. As you can also see from the figure, Inspiration is at the core. Intelligence is surrounding it, and finally, the consequence of these two is Intensity.

Ten Statements

Now let's take a look at the ten statements and understand how they map onto the three "i"s:

1. The purpose and vision of the company are clearly described and available to all team members.

2. The core values of the company are clear, understood, and followed by all team members.

3. The target customer profile of the company is clear and understood by all team members.

4. All team members can clearly describe the company's business.

5. The company successfully markets its products or services and regularly generates a large number of leads.

6. The company successfully and regularly converts a consistent percentage of leads into orders.

7. The company consistently delivers its products and services with high levels of customer satisfaction.

8. The company manages its cash and capital needs and meets all its obligations comfortably.

9. Teams meet regularly and experience high team member engagement and consistent follow through.

10. The leadership team has adequate time to discuss long-term challenges and put plans in place to address them.

Each of these ten statements is accompanied by a response template as follows:

10	9	8	7	6	5	4	3	2	1	0
Strongly Agree								Strongly Disagree		Don't Know

The higher the score, the more the individual agrees with the statement. A "Don't Know" is scored as a zero. So, for example, if a respondent were to strongly agree with any particular statement, he or she would circle a high number like 9 or 10. If he or she strongly disagreed, it would be a 1 or 2.

The diagnostic is designed for each of the "i"s to be captured by five of the statements as follows:

- ◇ *Inspiration*: Questions 1, 2, 4, 9, and 10
- ◇ *Intelligence*: Questions 3, 4, 7, 8, and 10
- ◇ *Intensity*: Questions 5, 6, 7, 8, and 9

Don't worry if this isn't making a whole lot of sense at the moment. We will review the example when we go back to Light Craft's story to explain this further.

Putting it all Together

After all the responses are gathered, they are entered into the *icube™ Diagnostic Analyzer* spreadsheet as shown in Table 2.1. You can download a copy of the *icube™ Diagnostic Analyzer* at http://pcsinsight.com/resources/. Alternatively, you can also have your team fill out the online diagnostic at http://pcsinsight.com/complimentary-assessment-form/. Our team will email you a completed diagnostic spreadsheet after all the answers have been received.

What Is the Diagnostic Looking for?

As described earlier, the *icube™ Diagnostic* is like a personality test for the organization. There are no right or wrong answers. Each of the ten statements is designed to capture a unique aspect of the organization as it relates to its Culture (Inspiration), Strategy (Intelligence), and Execution (Intensity). Furthermore, as the answers range from "Strongly Agree" to "Strongly Disagree" to "Don't Know," at its core, the diagnostic is capturing the pulse of the team collectively by aggregating individual responses. So, what we are actually looking for? The *icube™ Diagnostic* looks for two specific types of measures as it relates to the three "i"s:

Low and High Scores

A low score reflects the team member's perception that there is an opportunity for improvement in the area of focus for a particular statement. A high score reflects a perception that things are going well. Consistently low or high scores for statements and groups of statements that map to each of the three "i"s indicates that there is broad agreement within the team members in these areas.

Dispersion

Another measure that we look for is dispersion, or the variances between high and low scores. A high dispersion indicates a lack of agreement between team members on how they feel things are going. This is captured in the standard deviation measures in the *icube™ Diagnostic Analyzer*.

The ultimate objective of the *icube™ Diagnostic* is to help leadership teams get better insight into what is causing their teams to perform the way they are and to help them prioritize their actions so that they can address the most icube™ Diagnostic Analyzer

Company	LightCraft Innovations
Date	6/1/2016

Inspiration	25.00
Intelligence	28.46
Intensity	22.00

Total	654
Minimum Score	
Maximum Score	
Mean	
Std. Deviation	

				Topic	Purpose and Vision	Core Values	Customer Profile	Core Business	Marketing	Sales	Operations	Finance	Tactical Meetings	Strategic Meetings
					1	2	3	4	5	6	7	8	9	10
				Total	83	62	90	95	35	57	93	54	47	38
				Minimum Score	1	2	4	5	0	0	5	0	1	1
				Maximum Score	9	7	10	10	6	8	9	8	6	6
				Mean	6.38	4.77	6.92	7.31	2.69	4.38	7.15	4.15	3.62	2.92
				Std. Deviation	1.9	1.3	1.7	1.4	2.4	3.5	1.3	3.4	2.0	1.8
No	Respondent	Leader (Y/N)	M, S, O, F	Title										
1	Diana	Y	M,S,O	CEO	9	6	10	10	6	7	9	7	5	2
2	Jackie	Y	F	Office Mgr	6	5	8	8	5	8	9	8	6	5
3	Raj	Y	S,O	Sr. Designer	7	6	8	8	4	7	8	6	6	5
4	Theresa	Y	O	Tech. Spc.	8	5	9	9	6	8	9	7	5	4
5	Mike	Y	O	Proj. Mgr.	5	4	8	8	4	7	8	8	6	6
6	Tony	N	O	Asst. Designer	6	5	7	7	5	5	7	6	5	4
7	Lori	N	O	Asst. Designer	8	3	6	7	1	7	7	5	4	4
8	Gina	N	O	Asst. Designer	7	4	8	7	4	8	6	7	1	1
9	Noel	N	O	Asst. Designer	7	6	7	8	0	0	6	0	1	1
10	Marc	N	O	Asst. Designer	8	5	5	6	0	0	5	0	2	1
11	Nita	N	O	Asst. Designer	6	7	4	7	0	0	7	0	4	3
12	Jerry	N	O	Technician	5	4	5	5	0	0	6	0	1	1
13	Dmitry	N	O	Technician	1	2	5	5	0	0	6	0	1	1

Table 2.1: Light Craft Innovations' icube™ Diagnostic

important things first. It's also important not to get too hung up on the numbers and to use the *icube*™ *Diagnostic* as a general guide and not a precise measure of any kind. Now let's catch up with Diana to see what she learned about Light Craft through the diagnostic process.

Coffee Talk with Robert

The next week Diana went to Robert's office and settled into A2Z Distributing's well-appointed conference room. There was a handwritten note on the table from Robert to Diana: "Please bring up the spreadsheet on the projector. See you soon! - Robert" Diana brought out her laptop, hooked up to the conference room projector and displayed the *icube*™ *Diagnostic Analyzer* (Table 2.1) on the screen. A few minutes later Robert entered the room with a smile on his face. "Ah, there's the code to the secret of Light Craft's success!"

Diana smiled. "Well, you'd better tell me what this code is all about. Right now, it's all Greek and Latin to me, and all I know is a smattering of German!"

"Zer gut! Shall we jump right in?" asked Robert.

"Absolutely!"

Robert began by explaining how the statements mapped to the three "i"s of icube™, Inspiration, Intelligence, and Intensity. Then he clicked on several of the cells in the spreadsheet. When he was done, he looked up and said, "Now let's see what this is telling us about the team's experience at Light Craft. But before we do that, Diana, be sure to look at this as a baseline and not to interpret these scores absolutely. It's also important to keep in mind that this is a guide and not to overestimate the precision that these scores might imply. The goal here is to improve upon these numbers and focus on what is most important today. It's impossible for a company to do everything that might come out of such a diagnostic. In fact, you may have heard the notion that if everything is important, nothing is important! That's why I selected the few areas that I think are the most important for Light Craft today." Diana nodded in agreement.

Robert then hovered over the three scores to the left of the screen: Inspiration (25.00), Intelligence (28.46), and Intensity (22.00). "These are your aggregate scores. In an ideal company, all the scores would be 50. Personally, I think that's only theoretical. It would only happen if the company was functioning like the Borg in Star Trek. In a company with humans, I'd be happy to see a score or 35 or higher, again focusing more on improvement rather than an absolute score. What this is also telling you is that for Light Craft these scores are generally uniform with Intensity or execution having the highest opportunity for improvement followed by Inspiration or culture, and finally Intelligence or strategy. I'm actually not surprised by this because I know that you have excellent skills and know your stuff really well. Where the scores have suffered is in team inclusion. You are actually miles ahead of the team as we will see in the scores."

Diana was absorbing the contents of the spreadsheet with rapt attention. It was beginning to make sense. With a quickening pulse, she exclaimed, "I think I see where this is going!" Impressed by Diana's quick grasp of material, he continued.

"Now let's look at some of the other scores that I highlighted, what they mean and what they can tell us about Light Craft's team." He hovered his mouse on the numbers 35 and 0 in the Marketing column. "This is telling us that of all the aggregate scores, Marketing got the lowest, which was a zero. It's telling us that some team members don't know how the company markets its products, and more important, with a high of only 6, which I didn't highlight by the way, no one in the organization, including you, is satisfied by how Marketing is done. Similarly, you'll see a higher aggregate score for Sales (57) but a low score of 0."

He then pointed to the 3.5 in the Sales column. "That number is the standard deviation or a measure of the dispersion in the scores of sales effectiveness. That's telling us that some people are generally satisfied with the way sales are handled, and others have no idea how."

"Actually, that makes perfect sense. I've felt for a while now that we could be doing a lot better in marketing. I can also relate to the sales scores based on some of the emails I just responded to. Very interesting."

Diana and Robert continued discussing some of the other numbers and converged on three important priorities for Light Craft: 1) Improve team communication with more effective meetings, 2) Improve long-term planning and strategy development, and 3) Improve the company's marketing effectiveness. Diana immediately saw how these related to and could help resolve the issues she had listed before going through the diagnostic process. "So, Robert, is this something that you also did for A2Z?"

"Yes. I'll email you our diagnostic from when we first started. In our case, we were doing okay on execution, but we were horribly equipped to deal with any changes in the industry. The wake-up call was when we had a big change in the industry, and we were like deer in the headlights. I learned later that even though A2Z was successful, we really weren't a learning organization."

"A learning organization? What's that?"

"Something you will find out in the next phase of the icube™ journey. I'll email you some material that Pam Schaffer, our icube™ facilitator, shared with us. Read it, and let's get together after my trade-show in Vegas."

"Sounds good! Thanks again for all your time, Robert. Have a productive trip and see you when you get back." Diana packed up her things and reviewed everything that she had learned on the way back to the office.

Vision Track

- How are you feeling right now?
- Can you associate the different elements of your organization with the three "i"s?

Action Track To-Dos

- Review Table 2.1 and see if you can interpret the other scores that Robert highlighted. What about the ones that he didn't?
- Have your team take the diagnostic and list the insights you get for your company.

In the next chapter, we will dig deeper into icube™ and understand the elements of a learning organization.

SECTION 2: PLANNING AND BUDGETING

"By failing to prepare, you are preparing to fail."

—Benjamin Franklin

3: The Elements of a Learning Organization

"No, not magic. Months of teamwork!"

Light Craft in the Spotlight

As promised, Diana received an email from Robert with a presentation attached to it. Even though Diana was itching to open it and jump right in, she resisted the urge because she wanted this to be something that got her full attention. With everything else she had going on at that moment, she knew it would be unlikely. She did, however, open her calendar app and block out a couple of hours to review the information. Knowing that it wouldn't happen if she stayed in the office, she entered the name of the coffee shop in the location before saving it and went on with her day. Before we continue, take a moment to reflect on your action steps from the previous chapter.

Build Status Check-in

Vision Track

- ◇ How are you feeling now that you've taken some of the actions suggested in the previous chapter?
- ◇ Did your reflection raise additional questions or bring about more clarity?
- ◇ Are there any issues that you would like to add to your own issues list?

Action Track

- ◇ Have you completed all the to-dos from the previous chapter?
- ◇ Are there any issues that you need to address?
- ◇ What roadblocks did you encounter?
- ◇ If you didn't finish, what needs to happen in order for you to complete them?

Sources of Complexity

In our journey to understand the elements of a learning organization, our first stop is the concept of complexity. As an organization grows, it faces increasing complexity. Complexity is the state of *not being simple*. Something that is complex has many moving parts, is difficult to understand, and is difficult to fix when something goes wrong. In a business context, this means tough decisions and challenging problems. Most complexity boils down to three foundational outcomes:

1. Growing team size
2. Multiple market segments
3. Unbridled energy

Refer to Figure 3.1 for sources of complexity.

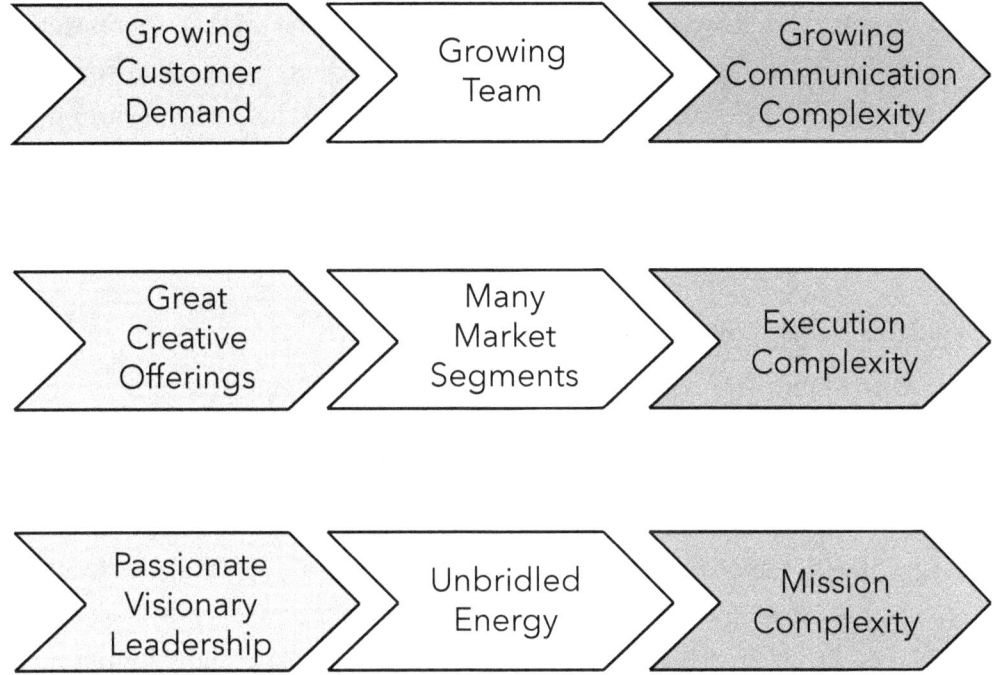

Figure 3.1: Sources of Complexity

You might notice that the outcomes listed above are not actually the root causes. In fact, for each of them, it is success itself that sows the seeds of increased complexity. Let's see how.

Success: The Root Causes of Complexity

1: *Growing Customer Demand*

In this case, when a company becomes successful, it starts needing more people to meet the demands of a growing customer base. As the company adds more people, this shoots up the complexity of communication. If you do the math, the number of two person conversations are proportional to the square of the number of people in a group. So, when there are three people, A, B, and C in a group, there are three conversations (AB, BC, and AC). A group of four people can have six possible conversations. But when you have twenty people in a group, the number of conversations between two people goes up to a whopping 190!

If you have ever played the game telephone in which one person whispers something into the ear of another person who then relays it to the next person, by the time it comes back to the first person, the message often bears no resemblance to what was said in the beginning. Every time the message is relayed to another person, the meaning can get distorted because the person receiving the message didn't hear or understand it correctly, or the person sending the message inadvertently changed the meaning in "translation." Similarly, separate but related conversations with similar "lost in translation" incidents can radically increase complexity many times over.

2: Great Creative Offerings
This occurs when an innovative company develops different successful products and product lines, resulting in many markets, thereby increasing the complexity of execution. Different markets and customer types have different norms and ways of doing business, and each must be supported to keep customers happy. While it's tempting to develop a wide range of products and services, it is often wiser to develop a smaller number of products that are wildly successful. There's a great video of Steve Jobs on YouTube that explains how saying no to many of Apple's potential initiatives is central to their strategy. https://www.youtube.com/watch?v=H8eP99neOVs

3: Passionate Visionary Leadership
This cause of complexity, which really arises from a combination of the other two, occurs when a hard-charging leader who has the entire strategy already mapped out in his or her head is driving the company. The path, the vision, and the steps to accomplish it, are often quite clear to these leaders because frankly they eat, sleep, and drink the business all day long. The problem is that while the team is charged up with unbridled energy, they are not quite clear what it all means or where they are going. Often this is because the leader isn't quite capable of, or for that matter interested in, actually communicating the vision and translating that into a mission. My observation is that such leaders use all their cognitive bandwidth on the big picture, the grand strategy, and while they appear to have the uncanny ability to see around corners, they can be alarmingly unable to clearly articulate the vision and the steps necessary to accomplish it. The outcome is lack of interest. That's why you may hear a charismatic leader say dismissively, "Don't bog me down with details. I described what I have in mind. Now figure out the way!" Unfortunately, however, as the adage goes, *the devil is in the details.*

When this happens, confusion abounds, and execution gets stifled, resulting in mission complexity.

If you've been in a company where this happens, you'll see that no one wants to challenge the leader on this because no one wants to look stupid. Each person thinks that every other person gets it but him or her. No one wants to be the one to speak up. And often if they do, the leaders shoot them down because, truth be told, the leaders haven't figured out a way to communicate it simply and clearly enough so that everyone, I mean *everyone*, right down to the maintenance crew, gets it. To boot, the big picture, visionary types often get impatient with the questions asked by those who are more detail oriented, let alone those who are not privy to all of the high-level meetings.

When I ask leaders of growing companies which scenario most applies to them, I get various responses such as one, one and two, or all three. The challenge for many leaders is that they are often unaware that they have not adequately communicated the vision. They think they have. And if asked, they will say, of course! More often than not, however, the vision is so clear in the eyes of these visionaries that they don't realize that others aren't getting it. This is a blind spot for them. The beauty of doing the *icube*™ *Diagnostic* in the beginning is that it provides employees a safe way to communicate how clearly they understand the vision. This can often be eye-opening for leaders. Since these situations occur naturally as a consequence of success, it's important for leaders not to blame themselves but to take notice and then take preventative action.

How Can Your Company Grow Like Wildfire but Manage Complexity?

Use icube™! Big surprise, right? The tools in this book will absolutely help you to manage and/or prevent problematic complexity from happening in the first place. Don't stop growing! Become the Apple of your industry's eye. Grow, grow, and grow some more. Just know you can avoid the pitfalls of growth along the way by implementing the principles and practices of icube™. Complexity is like the rust and grime that builds up over time in a smoothly running machine slowing it down and preventing it from doing its work. When you use icube™ to keep the company clean of the rust and grime of complexity, the work, or the output, which is the value generated by the company, shoots up. Let's see how.

The Essence of Value Creation

Let's take a detour to understand how value actually gets created by an organization. To do so, let's revisit the three layers of any organization from the outermost to the innermost:

1. Intensity
2. Intelligence
3. Inspiration

As you may recall, Inspiration, Intelligence, and Intensity are the three "i"s we introduced in the previous chapter. Refer to Figure 3.2.

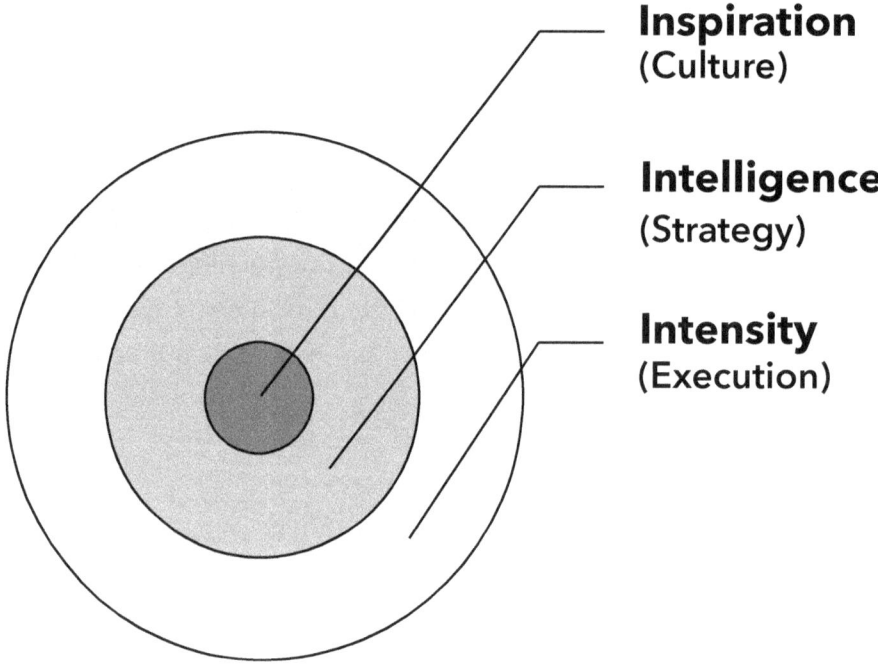

Figure 3.2: The Essence of Value Creation

In reality, every organization starts from the inside with Inspiration (culture) and moves outward to Intensity (execution), but I'm going to present them to you in reverse order because the execution of Intensity is concrete and clearly apparent whereas the culture of Inspiration is fuzzier. I have found that explaining the obvious and noticeable things first and then moving deeper into the underlying "why" helps people understand the concepts better, much like peeling an onion.

The outermost layer, Intensity, is the ability of the organization to execute actions and get things done. Think of your favorite restaurant or sports team that has a great reputation. When you see them in action, you are observing how they do what they do. In the case of the restaurant, you can observe a pattern of showing guests to their tables and presenting them with a menu. It may include a specific way in which the orders are taken and the food is brought out and presented. In the case of the sports team, you can observe the different plays they make or how team members collaborate, perhaps to pass a ball or a puck. This ability to act as a team and execute, which may be to deliver an excellent dining experience or win a game, is what I call Intensity.

However, Intensity doesn't occur automatically. For excellent execution, you need to have a great plan or playbook. In business terms, this is the strategy or Intelligence. This clearly defines what the team is going to do. The team can only execute well when they have a compelling strategy. In other words, excellent Intensity is the result of effective Intelligence.

Finally, effective strategies, or Intelligence, can only be developed if there is a core purpose behind it. We call this the Inspiration, and this is what drives the culture of the organization. Without a common purpose, and we shall see later, trust, the Intelligence of the company will not be effective. Thus, effective Intelligence is the consequence of clear and universally followed Inspiration.

Just so we are clear, this doesn't mean Inspiration can stand alone. The value generated by Intensity validates the Inspiration. I like to describe it as follows: Intelligence or strategy is inspired by Inspiration or culture; Intensity or execution is enabled by Intelligence; and Inspiration is sustained by Intensity. The three "i"s are deeply related and bound to each other.

You might notice how the diagnostic is designed to help uncover areas of improvement in these three areas. Now let's dig a little deeper into the three "i"s.

The icube™ Framework

The icube™ framework simplifies the three "i"s into their foundational elements. This time let's start at the core and work our way out.

Inspiration Defined

Inspiration is broken down into four foundational elements. The elements are follows:

1. Purpose
2. Vision
3. Values
4. Trust

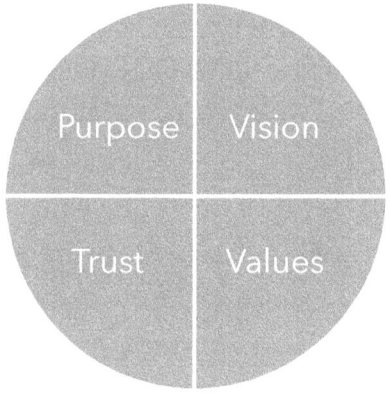

Figure 3.3 a: Inspiration

The way to understand this is as follows: Inspiration begins with a clear *purpose* for the organization to exist. This is the central reason that drives all of the organization's activities. This clear purpose then helps the team recognize the end-state when the purpose is realized. This is the *vision* that guides the activities of the team and what it should look like when the *purpose* is realized. The *purpose* and *vision* together help define the *values* or guiding principles that define how the team carries out its work. The *values* help create consistency in the actions and behaviors of team members.

Ultimately, *purpose, vision*, and *values* create trust, which is the binding glue of the organization. When there is a high level of trust, team members can count on their colleagues, and, in turn, be counted on by others. Cultures with high trust are capable of creating effective strategies or plans because these plans are driven by common purpose, vision and values shared by all team members.

Intelligence Defined

With a strong core of Inspiration, the organization can develop an effective Intelligence or strategy. Many experts have written about strategy. In icube™, we define strategy with six simple elements. Refer to Figure 3.3 b, Intelligence.

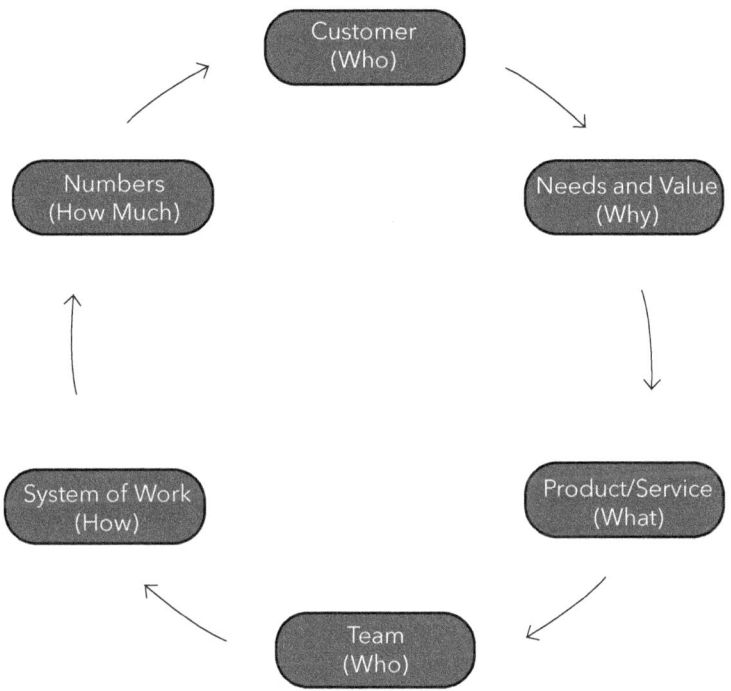

Figure 3.3 b: Intelligence

Intelligence comprises three external elements and three internal elements as follows:

External

1. Customer (Who)

2. Needs and Value (Why)

3. Product or Service (What)

Internal

4. Team (Who)

5. System of Work (How)

6. Numbers (How much)

Now let's take a look at each of these, starting with the external elements of Intelligence.

The Three External Elements of Intelligence

The customer (Who) is the organization's core constituent and defines the focal point of the purpose and vision. To understanding the customers, the team needs to identfy their profiles, interests, demographics, and behaviors. The next element of strategy is to understand what the customers need and value (Why). This defines the value proposition of the organization. After understanding the value proposition, the organization has to develop products and services (What) that deliver the value proposition to the customers. The first three elements of Intelligence are defined as the external elements of strategy and can be understood simply as the *who, why,* and *what*. We will be visiting these foundational elements in more detail in the icube™ sessions and workshops later on in the book.

The Three Internal Elements of Intelligence

After having defined the external elements of *who, why*, and *what*, we need the internal elements of *who, how,* and *how much*. We need a team (Who) that can develop and deliver products and services to our customers using efficient systems (How) that can be measured (How much) and assessed. Every team needs a System of Work comprised of efficient processes and tools in order to achieve consistently high-quality output. Then they need a defining a set of numbers (metrics) to measure the effectiveness of their systems. We will delve deeper into these foundational elements later in the book. Now let's look at Intensity.

Intensity Defined

When an organization defines its Inspiration and Intelligence clearly in this manner, the company is ready to execute its strategy to realize its mission as guided by its purpose. To understand Intensity, refer to Figure 3.3 c.

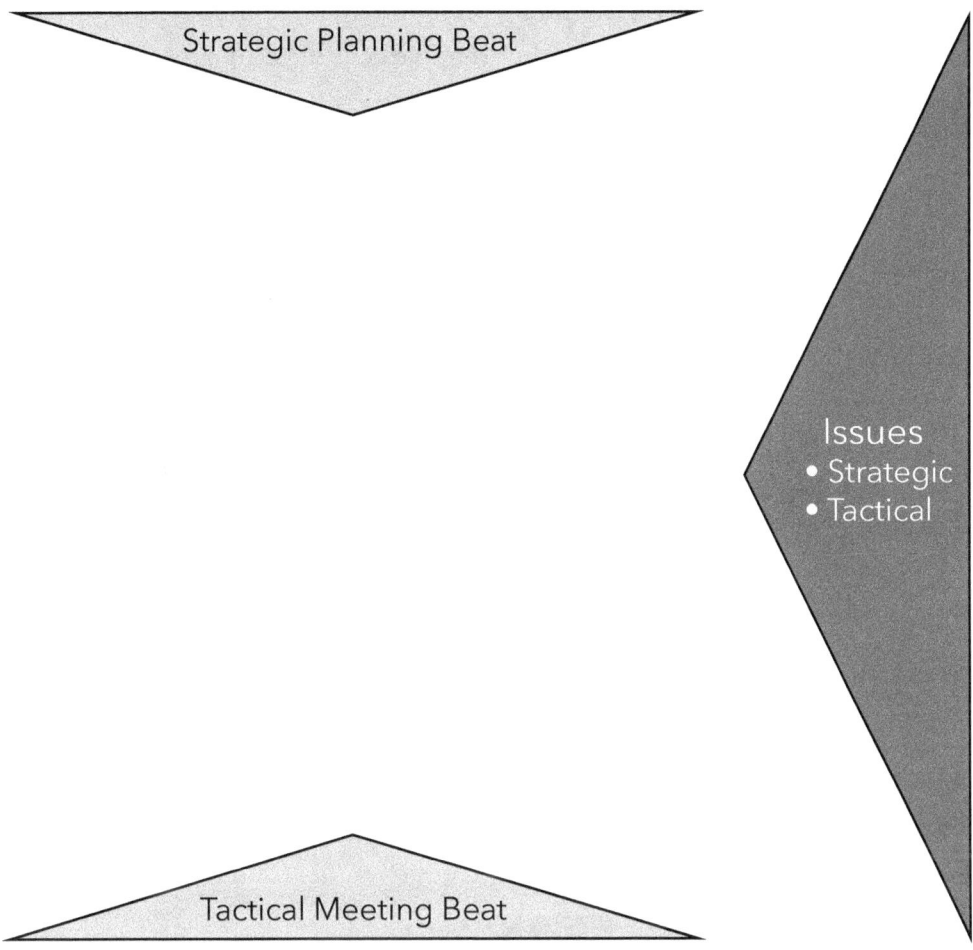

Figure 3.3 c: Intensity

When Inspiration and Intelligence are clear, Intensity, or execution, is largely a matter of getting things done. In the process of getting things done, the team will inevitably face obstacles or issues. However, the definition of Inspiration and Intelligence enable the obstacles or issues to become clear. These are depicted in the right-hand side of Figure 3.3 c. They are either long-term, big-picture issues that are strategic in nature or short-term, specific issues that are tactical in nature.

Intensity is the ability to execute the System of Work consistently while being able to resolve issues. Tactical issues can be resolved in a weekly tactical meeting beat. Strategic issues, on the other hand, can be resolved in effective, regular quarterly and annual strategic planning beats. By articulating, developing, and strengthening its Inspiration, Intelligence, and Intensity, any organization can embark on the path of long-term sustainable growth. It is only when we put all the three "i"s together that we get the complete icube™ framework as shown in Figure 3.4.

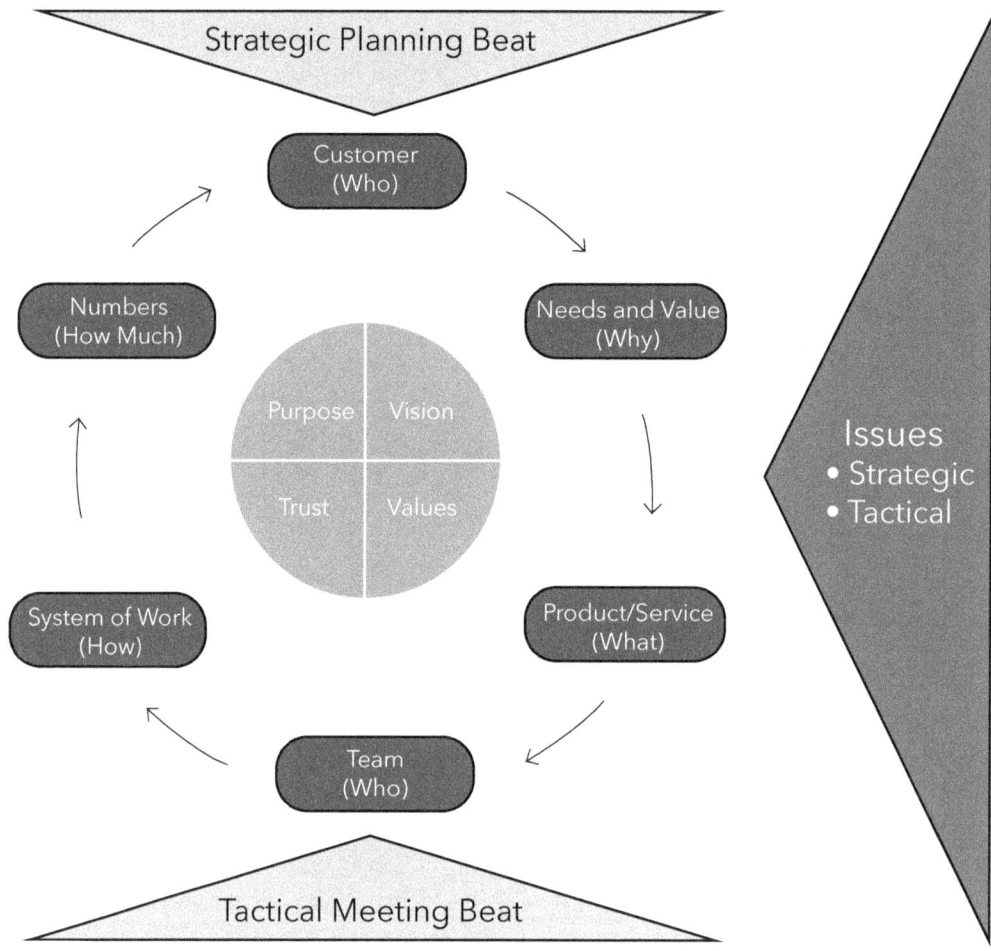

Figure 3.4: The icube™ Framework

You might want to bookmark this page so you can refer back to this graphic as necessary as you proceed through the book.

Why Trust?

Why is trust so critical? Starting from the top, whenever there is trust within a team, each team member knows the others have his or her back and can be counted on. This builds confidence. Confidence is absolutely essential for execution to be effective. Execution may or may not result in success. However, the knowledge that the team did its best enables it to analyze its performance and learn from the execution. This learning builds more trust and confidence to strengthen the organization even further. Refer to Figure 3.5.

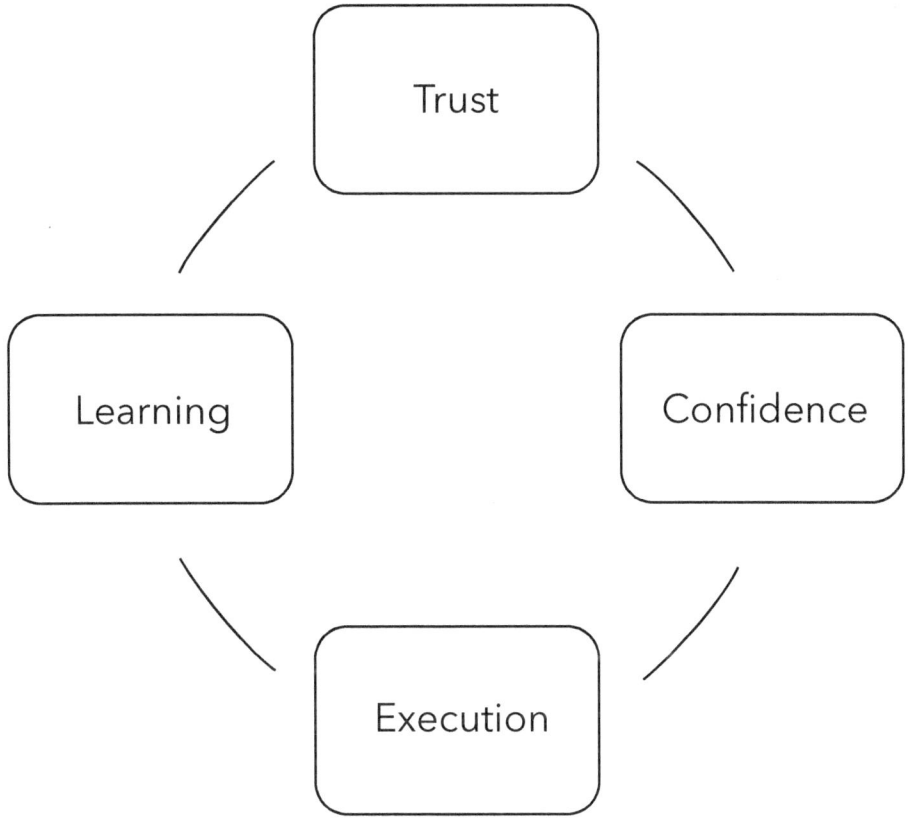

Figure 3.5: Why Trust?

Confidence and Arrogance

Let's take a look at what happens when learning either doesn't take place or stops happening and how it can impact trust. A note to make here before proceeding. The next graphic uses horizontal and vertical axes, a format I use often to illustrate concepts. I have found that comparing two dimensions is a good way to describe multiple scenarios and define the desirable state. In many cases this will be in the top right quadrant.

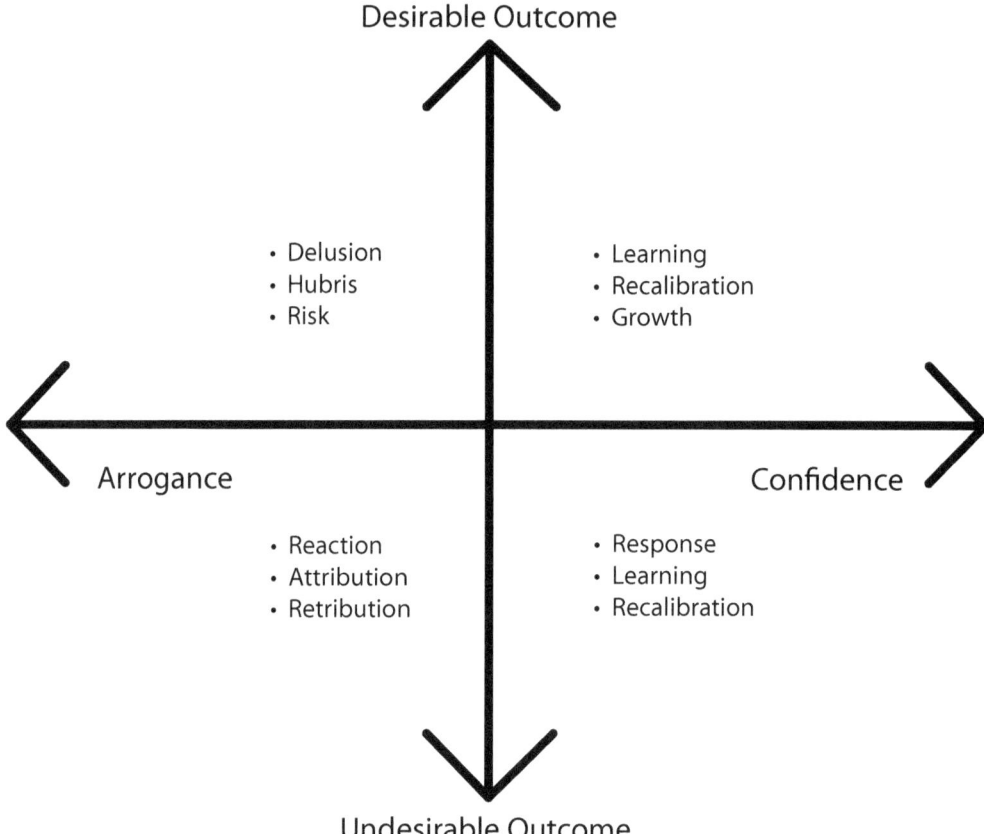

Figure 3.6: Confidence and Arrogance

The intent of this figure is to show how embarking on an initiative from a place of confidence versus arrogance can mean the difference between a desirable or undesirable outcome. I prefer to use the terms desirable and undesirable instead of the emotionally charged *success* and *failure*. I do this for two reasons. The obvious one is that failure, as we shall see later, can be a path to future success if the reasons for it are fully understood and can foster learning. The other subtler reason is that sometimes short-term successes can set a team down a path that may be harmful in the long run. By avoiding emotionally charged words, my hope is that we focus on making the journey itself a success regardless of the outcome.

What's the Difference Between Arrogance and Confidence?

Before we look at the quadrants, let's look at the attributes of Arrogance and Confidence. Arrogance is driven by a desire to outdo someone else and is founded in comparison. It is powered by ego and often perpetuated by unsubstantiated legends or stories. Confidence, on the other hand, is driven by a desire for improvement. It is powered by self-belief and developed by an objective understanding of the truth. Now let's look at how arrogance or confidence can impact outcomes.

How Does Arrogance vs. Confidence Impact Outcomes?

When an arrogant organization encounters a setback, first there is a *reaction*. By reaction I mean something that occurs without any deliberation or thought. An example of a reaction is what you might experience when you get some completely unexpected news that may be good or bad. Let's say, for example, that a company is field testing a new product after all internal testing is complete. It would probably need the help of a customer to carry out the test for them. An arrogant organization would most likely oversell the product and pay no attention to the risk that the customer might be taking in testing the product. If something bad were to happen, it would perhaps react by firing the people who delivered the product to the customer before even finding out what happened. This is because arrogant organizations do not expect any kind of bad news and are hence unprepared. The reaction is soon followed by an intent to lay blame on someone or something. Blame is then followed by retribution. When this happens, the trust in the organization shrivels, and it becomes increasingly ineffective at executing.

If an arrogant organization achieves a desirable outcome, it often becomes deluded as to the reasons for the outcome. The delusion is followed by hubris in which all caution is thrown to the wind. Ultimately, the organization may try to take on more than it can chew and in the process, destroy itself.

On the other hand, when a confident organization is dealt a setback, or an undesirable outcome, the first thing it does is to *respond*. A response is a planned handling of an undesirable but potentially expected situation. In our example above, a confident organization would first set appropriate expectations for the trial. Additionally, it would work closely with the customer to ensure that the test isn't subjecting the customer's business or assets to risk. Finally, it would craft out an action plan ahead of time in case something bad should happen so that it can respond quickly if need be. In everyday life, having a well-trained fire department in a city is an example of having a response in place. This is also why fire fighters are called first responders when there is an accident. Confident team leaders are aware that things may not go as planned, and they have a premeditated response to the situation. The response is followed by learning to understand the causes of the outcome, which is then followed by recalibration to set up for another attempt, if they get a second chance, or to do things differently with the next similar situation, all amidst an environment of high trust.

Just so we are clear, this is not to imply that we expect the team to have answers and planned responses for every single unfortunate event that might befall the company. More so it is to foster a culture and type of thinking that is tolerant of measured risk taking and risk mitigation without personalizing success or failure. One of my favorite examples of a company highlighting failures and staying humble is the global venture capital firm Bessemer Venture Partners (https://www.bvp.com). Easily accessible on its website is a page that they call the "Anti-Portfolio" (https://www.bvp.com/portfolio/anti-portfolio). It lists all the companies the firm declined to invest in over the years that subsequently enjoyed huge successes, like Google and Facebook among others. If you know anything about the egos of venture capitalists, I think you will agree with me that this is highly unusual, and I give them credit.

As they say on their website, ". . . . [the list] inspires us in our ongoing endeavors to build growing businesses." It is also important to realize that the reasons they passed on some of these investments varied, and at the time the decision was made, they may not have had all the information. In other words, all of these decisions might have been the right ones in light of what was known at that time. This is the key learning here. You can make the right decision and still not have the best outcome. However, if you look at their track record, they are a highly successful firm and are clearly making more decisions that yield a positive outcome than the other way around.

Over time, the cycle of learning and recalibration can help move outcomes from undesirable to desirable. Even when a confident organization gets a desired outcome, the first thing it does is to learn because sometimes the assumptions made at the start of a project may be incorrect, and the learning prevents misconceptions from taking root. The learning is then followed by recalibration as before. When an organization follows this pattern, over time it will result in much lower risk growth, as shown in Figure 3.6.

The central idea in this illustration is that most organizations will start somewhere in the middle of the horizontal axis. However, only through holding an organization-wide attitude of learning will it become a confident organization with trust in abundance. This is the core concept of the icube™ philosophy. As I alluded to earlier, being able to respond to situations is central to the concept of learning. And being able to respond requires having a sophisticated ability to manage and understand risk. In the next section, we will see how learning organizations are able to do that effectively.

Navigating Risk

Navigating risk is a challenge for every leadership team in a growing organization. Risk occurs when leaders don't have enough information to make a decision. In this complex world of ours, it is often humanly impossible to have all the information. Some forces are beyond our control and bring forth the uncertainty that can have a real impact on us directly or indirectly. Sometimes risk is easy to see, and other times it isn't. Let's use another two-dimensional graphic to illustrate this. This concept was described in the May 31, 2015, *Forbes* magazine article by John Carpenter, entitled, "Boston Beer Company's Jim Koch on the Difference between Dangerous and Scary." Jim Koch, founder of the Boston Brewing company, says, "There are things in life that are scary, but not dangerous, but we're scared of them. And then there are things that are dangerous, but not scary. And those are the real problem." Refer to Figure 3.7.

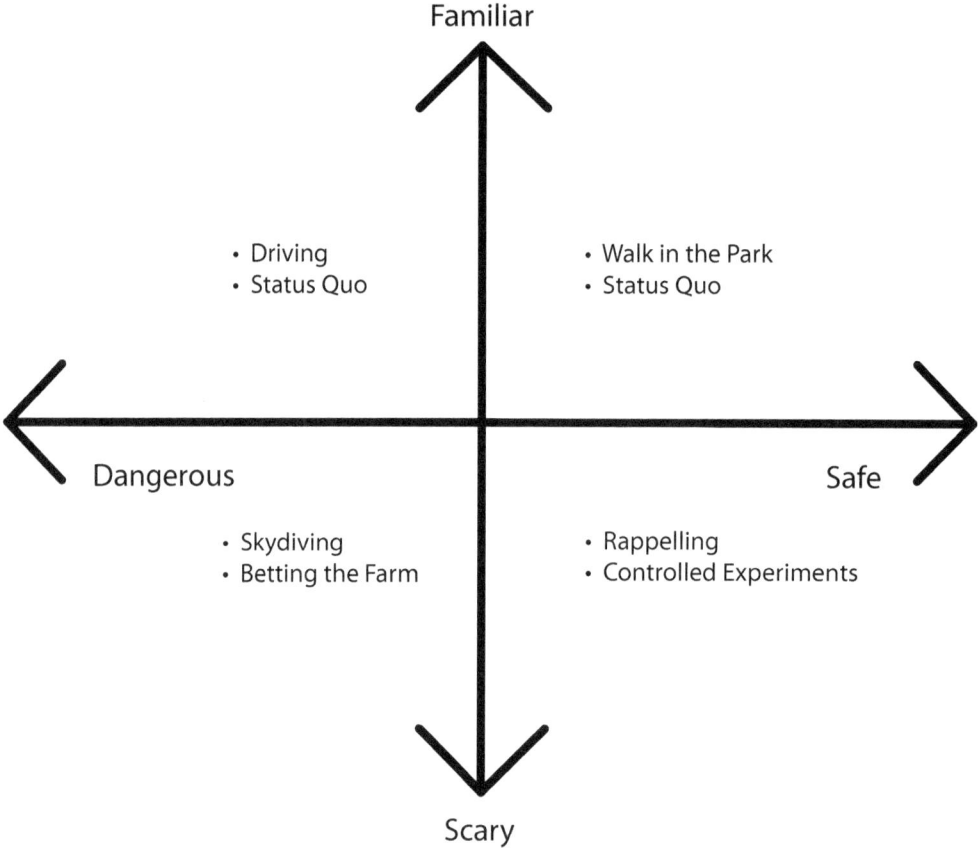

Figure 3.7: Navigating Risk

When we consider taking an action, we usually know if it is inherently dangerous or safe. This is the horizontal axis. On the other hand, it may be familiar or it may be scary. That's the vertical axis.

The top right quadrant involves activities that are both familiar and safe such as a walk in the park. In the business context, the status quo of day-to-day activities is also familiar and safe.

The bottom left quadrant is also straightforward. This includes activities that we know are dangerous *and* scary, like skydiving. Similarly, in business, taking on enormous financial risk with an uncertain outcome is scary and dangerous as it could easily put a company out of business if things don't work out.

The tricky quadrant is the one on the top left. This encompasses activities that can actually be dangerous but don't appear as such, like driving on the freeway. In business, depending on the external environment, the status quo may be familiar but actually very dangerous. History is littered with examples of companies that kept doing things the same way while the world around them changed. Eventually, they found themselves to be irrelevant and in an untenable situation. One example of this is Kodak Corporation, which was actually the company that invented the digital camera and dominated the camera film business. Yet even as it saw signs of other companies making and selling digital cameras, it continued to hold on to the contracting film business. Today it still exists, but is a fraction of the size it once was.

That brings us to the last quadrant of that which is scary but actually quite safe, like rappelling down the side of a cliff if done properly. But depending on how high off the ground you are, it can be pretty scary. In the business context, doing controlled experiments that are outside the scope of day-to-day work can be scary, but if done right, can be quite safe. These experiments can often lead the way for a company to respond to market conditions and change the way it conducts business, thus helping it to stay relevant. In fact, the company that was Google renamed itself Alphabet, Inc. so that it could separate out its controlled experiments from the core search engine business. As it states on its website, "You could expect us to make 'smaller' bets in areas that might seem very speculative or even strange when compared to our current businesses." Perhaps if Kodak had used some of its excess capital to make some controlled experiments in digital camera technology, it might have been a leader in the space. Now that we have examined all the elements of a learning organization and the icube™ framework, let's check back in with Diana and Light Craft.

Coffee Talk with Robert

With Robert out on his trip, Diana used the time to understand the material that he had sent her. She started mapping out the different areas and practices of her company to the icube™ framework. After she was done, she could clearly see how the dots connected. She also felt like she knew what Light Craft Innovations needed to look like. Her mind, however, was full of the question, *how do we get there?*

Vision Track

- How are you feeling right now?
- Can you relate the different elements of the three "i"s to your organization?

Action Track To-Dos

- Review Figure 3.4 and use it to map out the areas and practices of your organization.
- Take the afternoon off and see how many of the elements of icube™ you can successfully articulate as they relate to your company.

Becoming a learning organization requires a step-by-step approach. In the next chapter, we will review the journey to becoming a learning organization.

4: The Journey

"I guess a map would've been handy right about now."

Light Craft in the Spotlight

Now that she knew *what* her company's diagnostic needed to look like and how it should act, Diana was curious to know *how* to get there. With that thought, she reviewed the next section in the materials that Robert had given her before leaving on his trip. But first, let's take a moment to check in on your own experience using the *Build Status Check-in* below.

Build Status Check-in

Vision Track

- ◇ How are you feeling now that you've taken some of the actions suggested in the previous chapter?

- ◇ Did your reflection raise additional questions or bring about more clarity?

- ◇ Are there any issues that you would like to add to your own issues list?

Action Track

- ◇ Have you completed all the to-dos from the previous chapter?

- ◇ Are there any issues that you need to address?

- ◇ What roadblocks did you encounter?

- ◇ If you didn't finish, what needs to happen in order for you to complete them?

Steps Along the icube™ Journey

In the earlier chapter, we reviewed the elements of a thriving, learning organization by using the icube™ framework (See Figure 3.4). We saw the three "i"s, Inspiration, Intelligence, and Intensity, through the series of Figures 3.3 a, 3.3 b, and 3.3 c. In this chapter, we take a big picture view of the journey that will develop each of these elements for your business. Think of this chapter as the itinerary for your journey. In subsequent chapters, we will delve into the specific stops along the way to get into the "how." When you first look at the icube™ journey, you'll notice a couple of things right away. One, there are five steps, and two, they follow a certain pattern. Refer to Figure 4.1.

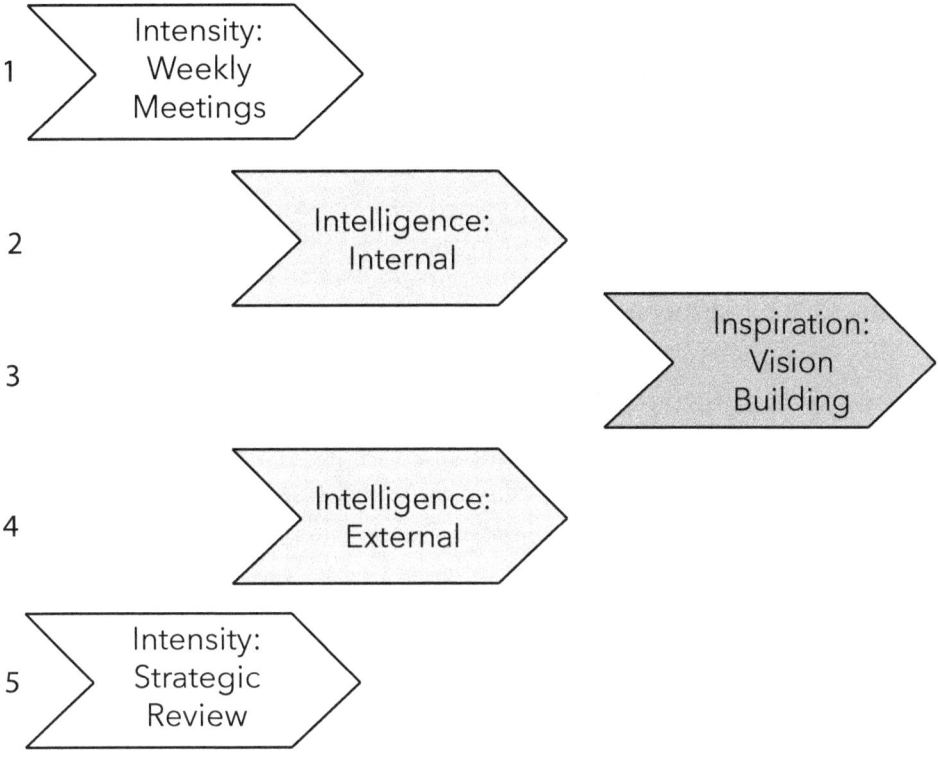

Figure 4.1: Steps in the icube™ Journey

You will notice that the steps follow a sideways V-shape relative to the depth of the "i"s of icube™ (Figure 3.2) This appears counter intuitive at first but becomes clear when we look at it this way. The three "i"s of icube™, Inspiration, Intelligence, and Intensity, are actually part of the same whole. To get to the core or Inspiration, we must first start by developing a basic framework for how to work as a team. This is covered in the first two steps. Then in steps three and four, we learn how to articulate the vision and communicate it externally. Finally, we learn how to put it all together and convert the learning into follow-up actions.

What Is Covered in Steps 1-5?

A trained facilitator guides the team through the icube™ steps with the following sessions and workshops:

1. Intensity Day Morning Session
2. Intensity Day Afternoon Session
3. Vision Building Workshop
4. Positioning and Branding Workshop
5. Quarterly Review Session

Now let's dig a bit deeper and look at what is covered in each of these steps.

Steps 1 and 2: Intensity Day

This is the official kick-off of the icube™ process. The proverbial train leaves the station here, and assuming it stays on track, this is the start of the team working in a fulfilling, productive environment. The team receives a set of tools on Intensity Day they can use for the rest of the journey and beyond.

Intensity Day begins with the sources of complexity, the genesis of most organizations, and an understanding of workflow and the metrics behind it. It also covers some elements of Intensity and Intelligence. For Intensity, the team learns how to conduct effective tactical meetings and how to manage strategic and tactical issues. For the internal elements of Intelligence, the team develops a Functional Framework and a System of Work audit, which reveals bottlenecks in the organization, followed by a compilation of an initial set of numbers.

After Intensity Day, the team schedules regular tactical meetings, usually weekly in perpetuity. Over the following weeks, it learns how to raise the accountability of team members to resolve issues and execute its quarterly wildly important goals (WIGs). This alone is such a significant change that even though we haven't even arrived at the next station in our icube™ journey, team members feel a powerful shift in their experience.

Step 3: Vision Building Workshop

After a few weeks of getting used to having tactical meetings that are engaging and result in a high level of accountability, the next stop in the journey is the Vision Building Workshop. The goal of this workshop is to conduct a, "Where are we?" situational review and use that to guide the team in answering some key questions as it defines the foundation of its Inspiration. The specifics are described in detail in Chapter 7. When the team is done, it has a mission statement, a list of core values, and a long-term vision statement. In addition to these, the team also describes the three-year picture and any key quantifiable factors, a one-year picture, and a set of annual WIGs (wildly important goals).

Step 4: Positioning and Branding Workshop

Immediately following the Vision Building Workshop, the team conducts its companion, the Positioning and Branding Workshop. It is usually on the same day to ensure continuity and ease of scheduling. Whereas the former is related to the Inspiration of the team, the latter is focused on the external elements of Intelligence.

The objective of this workshop is for the team to get clarity on and a unified understanding of the customer. The team also converges on a shared agreement of the brand essence, the brand challenge, and how the organization wishes to represent itself in the world. The team can then hand over the deliverables of this workshop to the internal or external marketing team in order to define and execute strategy and tactics so they can attract the right type of customer leading to authentic marketing and promotion.

Step 5: Quarterly Strategic Review Session

Approximately ninety days after the first internal Intensity Day, the team reconvenes for the external part of Intensity, the Quarterly Strategic Review. Having completed all the other elements of icube™, this session takes a long-term view of the organization and tackles the strategic issues it is facing. In this session, the team reviews the elements of Inspiration, Intelligence, and Intensity, conducts a team health and trust review as described later in the book, and sets to-dos or WIGs for the following week or quarter.

Rinse and Repeat

After the first Quarterly Strategic Review, the team has completed one icube™ cycle, the first step in a life-long journey of improvement and excellence. From here on out, the team continues with its tactical meetings and Quarterly Strategic Reviews. Along the way, the team can revisit its mission, vision, positioning, and branding as often as needed. I recommend that it review these at least annually.

In addition, every subsequent fourth quarterly session, the first one roughly coinciding with the anniversary of Intensity Day, is the Annual Review in which the team reviews and updates the one-year and three-year pictures and sets annual WIGs along with quarterly WIGs and to-dos. For example, let's say we had Intensity Day on January first. The first quarterly review would be on or around April first, the second one on or around July first, the third one on or around October first, and the first annual review on or around the following January first, thus completing one whole year of icube™.

Once the leadership team is comfortable with the icube™ process, the facilitator or a trained team member can move on to sharing it with the departments. This is done layer by layer eventually encompassing the entire organization. There is no set time frame prescribed for this. As long as the organization continues to take steady and deliberate steps, excellence is absolutely achievable. Safe travels!

Coffee Talk with Robert

After settling into their usual spots at the coffee shop, Diana was prepared to pick Robert's brain.

"So how was the trip?" asked Diana.

"Surprisingly productive!" replied Robert. "It was one the regional tradeshows that A2Z attends. I was there with a couple of our team members. We had some great vendor rapport building moments, and during the down time we were able to discuss some ideas for the business. Nice thing is that we have recorded a bunch of promising ideas in the issues list on our quarterly review board."

"Is that the icube™ review you mentioned before?"

"Exactly. We have one coming up a few weeks from now. I'm looking forward to it!"

"Robert, that is so not like you! You've always hated meetings," Diana said with a smile.

"Yep. It's been a sea change for me since we implemented icube™. I guess I know that whenever we have a tactical meeting or icube™ session, things get done. My execution oriented brain gets a little dopamine hit just thinking about it. Anyway, what's up with you? How are things at Light Craft? Did you have a chance to review the materials I sent?"

"Light Craft continues to be crazy. That's not a complaint, by the way. It does keep me busy. And yes, I did review all the materials. Very cool stuff! Dare I say that I no longer feel crazy or inadequate like I was feeling before?"

"I get it," Robert replied. "I remember when we did the diagnostic and then related A2Z to the icube™ graphic, I sensed a confidence in me that I hadn't felt in years as a businessman. Instead of feeling lost and unsure of how to lead the team, I began to understand the sources of our troubles and how to fix them. The moment I saw that I was convinced we needed to go forward."

"That helps. I think I'm in the same boat you were then. But you know me. I don't jump into things as quickly as you do. Can we talk a little about your experience?"

"Sure, and since you brought it up, my jumping into things hasn't always proven to be the best thing. Sometimes I wonder how I can be more deliberate like you, Diana!"

"Looks like we're both having a 'grass is greener on the other side' moment!" said Diana. "Okay, I guess my biggest concern is that I won't have the time to do this. But I know you're not the most patient person when it comes to systems and structures, so how did you make time for this? Second, how did you change your mindset to be accepting of the disruption?"

"I'll answer the second question first," said Robert. "I was at a particularly vulnerable point in my experience as a business owner. Yes, A2Z was successful, but things weren't as fun as they used to be. The crisis that precipitated all of this didn't help. So I didn't need much of a push to change my mindset. To answer the second question, our facilitator, Pam, managed everything. It felt like the whole team was being taken on a trip with a very capable tour guide. I was concerned about the time spent in one more meeting, but Pam is such an amazing facilitator and 'accountability extractor' that pretty soon the team fell in line, including me, and from that point on, it has become the new way of doing business. And the icube™ Trello boards reduce extra time in managing or administering the process to nearly nothing. Does that answer your question?"

"Yes, it does. One follow-up question. You guys used Pam to help with the facilitation. From what I read in the materials, a team can self-facilitate the system. Did you ever consider that?"

"We did, but pretty soon it became clear to me that we didn't have the skills to do that internally. I certainly don't have them. Also, we were in the middle of the business issue, and considering this was something new to us, I thought it best to invest in the professional services of an external facilitator. Looking back, I think that was the right decision. From a return on investment standpoint, icube™ has paid for itself many times over, including returning the joy of running my business again."

"One thing to consider though, Diana," continued Robert, "is that your company is more organized than ours has ever been, so it may be realistic for Light Craft to self-facilitate. I wouldn't rule that out completely." (Note: We will discuss whether or not a company should self-facilitate or hire a professional facilitator in the next chapter and in the last section of the book.)

"That makes sense. I'll give that some thought," Diana agreed. "So how did your team respond? Did they think that this was one of Robert's wild goose chases?"

"You know me and my team pretty well, Diana!" said Robert with a chuckle. "There was a bit of that for sure. But two things happened that tipped the scales in the favor of icube™. The team could see that it offered the structure and form that they had been craving. They also saw it as a way to keep my wild goose chases in check. I still propose them, but now we have a better system to decide as a team which ones we should actually go after. After Pam did an introductory meeting with the team, even the skeptics were convinced. She is quite talented as a facilitator and knows how to read a room and get the most out of everyone participating."

Diana reflected for a moment and then finally said, "I need to consider the pros and cons of using professional services versus self-facilitation, but for sure, we're going to do this thing."

"I was hoping you would say that, Diana! This is going to be transformational for Light Craft. In six months, you won't know how you were running your business before. Tell you what, while you're thinking about whether or not to use a professional facilitator, let's schedule a time for me to meet with your team and answer any questions they may have. How's that sound?"

"Absolutely fabulous, Robert! Thank you. It's a deal!" With that our duo picked up their belongings and left. Now let's check in with you to see how your journey is coming along.

Vision Track

- How are you feeling right now?
- Can you visualize the experience of facilitating icube™ within your organization?

Action Track To-Dos

- Review Figure 4.1 with the rest of your team.
- Compile a list of pros and cons of using a professional facilitator versus self-facilitating icube™ for your company.

In the next section and chapter, we will get ready for the train to leave the station and jump right into Intensity Day!

SECTION 3: DEMOLITION

"Change is disturbing when it is done to us, exhilarating when it is done by us."

—Rosabeth Moss Kanter

5: Intensity Day

Intensity Day Part 1: Morning

"John, why are you saying you don't know where you fit in?"

Light Craft in the Spotlight

While driving back to the office after her meeting with Robert, Diana found her mind racing with some of the concepts she had learned. She smiled to herself when it dawned on her that these were not really new concepts. In fact, she noted that many of them were things she had read or heard about. For the first time, though, she saw a path to implement these really exciting ideas.

Soon after she met with Light Craft's core leadership team, comprised of Jackie Davis, Jerry Lin, Mike Burns, Raj Patel, and Theresa Janovic, to share information about icube™ and get their feedback. There were many questions and a wide range of emotions from hope, intrigue, and fear to skepticism.

She then asked Robert to come meet with her team as someone they respected who had gone through the process. He graciously agreed.

The group assembled a few days later in Light Craft's conference room early on a Friday so it would be a relaxed environment. Diana opened the discussion by thanking Robert for his time and gave him the floor. He started off by quickly reviewing the core components of the icube™ system and the journey that Diana had learned a few days earlier. Then he opened up the discussion and solicited questions from the group. The first question came from Mike.

"Robert, thanks for making your time available to us today. We really appreciate it. One of the concerns is if we will have the time to manage everything and add in yet another weekly meeting. Can you share your experiences on this with the team?"

"That's actually the first question I had when we facilitated icube™ at A2Z," replied Robert. "If you know anything about me, it's that I used to hate meetings with a passion. I am what they call a classic 'promoter.' We like to get things done quickly, and unnecessary gatherings irritate the heck out of us. I learned, however, as will you, that this was because we weren't running meetings properly. But icube™ will help make your meetings both excellent and energizing. You will actually spend less time in meetings because they are so effective."

"I believe that, Robert," said Raj. "At my previous company, our team leader was great at running meetings. She kept things on track, and we were all very thankful for that. My question, though, is about the business itself. A2Z is a distribution business. Here at Light Craft we do custom design work. Will icube™ work in our environment?"

"Excellent question, Raj!" said Robert. "Before I answer that, however, a comment on your observation. While your previous team leader might have had some innate abilities, icube™'s tools and practices will help anyone run effective meetings if he or she follows the process. See icube™ is not really about business. It's about people. So it doesn't matter what your business model is. It's a way to enhance collaboration and alignment and reduce internal friction."

The team continued with several other questions related to clarifications about icube™ and the journey. After feeling comfortable that all the questions had been answered, Diana suggested that the team schedule an Intensity Day session for Light Craft. Everyone agreed and Diana volunteered to call Pam Schaffer, the icube™ facilitator who was also working with Robert's team at A2Z.

Build Status Check-in

Vision Track

- ◇ How are you feeling now that you've taken some actions suggested in the previous chapter?
- ◇ Did your reflection raise additional questions or bring about more clarity?
- ◇ Are there any issues that you would like to add to your own issues list?

Action Track

- ◇ Have you completed all the to-dos from the previous chapter?
- ◇ Are there any issues that you need to address?
- ◇ What roadblocks did you encounter?
- ◇ If you didn't finish, what needs to happen in order for you to complete them?

Goals of Intensity Day

As described in the icube™ journey earlier, the goal of Intensity Day is to get a team started with Intensity and the internal elements of Intelligence. Intensity is comprised of the Tactical Meeting Beat and the Strategic Meeting Beat. The internal elements of Intelligence are as follows: System of Work, the Team, and Numbers.

In addition, the company also starts using the software Trello (www.trello.com). Trello is a collaboration system that organizes projects into boards, lists, and cards. The inspiration for Trello is Kanban, a scheduling system developed at Toyota Motor Corporation in the 1950s to visually represent inventory flows, improve production throughput, and accomplish Just In Time (JIT) inventory management.

Kanban's design makes it an elegant, visually powerful, and user-friendly system. The creators of Trello have taken these concepts and converted them into a highly visual, easy-to-use system that makes implementing icube™ easy and effective, especially the meeting beats. This is as good a time as any to state that my company PCS Insight doesn't have any financial or strategic interest in Trello™ or the company that owns it. As such we cannot guarantee if it will work for you or your company. There are many other solutions that use the Kanban design, and it would be easy and straightforward to implement icube™ templates in these tools and use them instead.

Preparing for the Session

Intensity Day is the first step in the process of implementing icube™ for a business. Starting off well can make big difference in the quality of the experience and its effectiveness for the team. Since it can be quite "intense," there are two important things to which the team leader should pay attention: location and facilitation.

Location

Ideally, the team should do this at an off-site location. It gets team members out of their routine and helps them be present and less subject to distractions. If you do choose to use an off-site location, ensure it is easy to get to, quiet, comfortable, adaptable for team interactions, has good lighting, a whiteboard or flip chart and markers, and technology such as a good computer display system and Internet access.

The facilitator should inspect the location ahead of time to ensure that everything is in place before the session. There should be no surprises so that the team can start as soon as everyone has arrived.

Facilitation

Since icube™ is a facilitated process, it's important that your facilitator has excellent facilitation skills to ensure a high level of team participation and engagement. It is also important that the facilitator be familiar with the content ahead of time.

If you haven't facilitated group discussions before, it's a great idea to spend time learning some basic skills before attempting to facilitate an icube™

session. While a deep dive into facilitation skills is not the core focus of this book, here are some of the main responsibilities of a facilitator:

1. Comfort

   A good facilitator makes all participants feel comfortable, welcomed, and valued. They also need to give the group breaks as needed so that participants can attend to potential distractions and maintain a high energy level.

2. Participation and engagement

   The facilitator is the traffic cop during group meetings. It is his or her responsibility to encourage even and engaged participation from the whole group.

3. Conflict management

   While the facilitator doesn't necessarily avoid or encourage conflict, it is his or her responsibility to ensure that it is about ideas and not personalities.

4. Observation

   A big part of the facilitation process is observing the group dynamics and looking for signs of behavior that could undermine the quality of the discussion.

5. Guidance and focus on value

   The facilitator guides the group to accomplish session goals using tools like the Issues List to keep the session on track while not losing sight of important items that come up in discussions.

6. Managing group dynamics

   Finally, the facilitator has to ensure that the group dynamics reflect high levels of trust, engagement, and participation. A facilitator must have the judgement to call out problem behavior at the right time.

It is best if you can get an external facilitator. This allows all team members to participate. There are a couple of ways to do this. You might find an icube™ buddy company: you facilitate their sessions and someone from that company facilitates yours. The other way to do this is to contact PCS Insight, LLC (www.pcsinsight.com) and see if a professional facilitator is right for your company.

It's also best if the most influential leader such as the owner or general manager not be the facilitator unless there is already a high level of trust in the team. Even if it's just for the session, the facilitator has a lot of influence on the group. Hence, it is best that this role be played by someone who isn't normally in a power position. This way it is more likely that the rest of the team will be more comfortable and the participation more authentic. As you might guess, good facilitators are "people" people and excellent readers of nonverbal cues.

Agenda of Intensity Day

The actual Intensity Day session can take anywhere from a few hours to a whole day, depending on the state and size of the team and the alignment that already exists. Most teams can cover the following agenda comfortably during the course of a business day if the facilitator keeps the discussion on track:

1. Check-in
2. System of Work
3. Team
4. Numbers
5. Meeting Beats
6. WIGs
7. Issues List Review: Tactical/Strategic
8. Trello Setup Plan
9. Closing

You'll notice that there isn't any set time for any of these topics. This is intentional as the time it takes to cover any individual item varies from team to team and business to business. Some businesses are very quick at reviewing their System of Work and need to spend more time on people issues. Others are just the opposite.

A good facilitator monitors the progress and uses the Issues List to keep the session on track. Along the same lines, while conclusion of each item is a logical break point, the facilitator should look for opportunities to give the team breaks to stretch and rejuvenate. On average a short (five minutes or so) break every ninety minutes is a good pace. In addition, plan on having a longer break for lunch and one midafternoon, a couple of hours after lunch, for coffee or refreshments. With that, let's dig right into the agenda and take each of these elements one at a time. At the conclusion of this exercise, you will be ready to facilitate your own Intensity Day.

Check-in

As the first step in the session, the Check-in establishes the mood. There are four important items for the facilitator to cover:

1. Ground rules

   First, establish ground rules for the session and team behavior. This covers the need for all participants to be present, engaged, and enthusiastic. The group decides how frequently they will take breaks, how to manage distractions, and how they will make the session a success.

2. Expectations

   Next, the facilitator goes around the room and asks participants what their expectations are for the session. These are listed on a whiteboard or flip chart and retained for the duration of the session so that they can be reviewed at the end.

3. Logistics

   After this, the team reviews the logistics and facility details such as location of restrooms, arrangement for refreshments and lunch, and any other items necessary.

4. Issues list

   Finally, the facilitator uses the Issues List tool to capture tangential but important items that are not on the agenda. The facilitator uses this tool vigilantly throughout the icube™ process. The Issues List is prominently displayed throughout the entire session and reviewed for classification before its conclusion.

System of Work

Everything we have covered so far helps lay the foundation for the session. Now we delve into the inner workings of the business by examining one of the internal elements of Intelligence, the System of Work.

1. Cycle of execution
2. System of Work audit
3. Prioritization

This is the first opportunity for the team to look at their company as a sophisticated mechanism with moving parts that responds to customer demand by creating a product or service to meet that demand. Another way to look at it is to see it as combination of a System of Work having a specific input and generating an output. To understand that better, the first concept that we cover is the Cycle of Execution.

1. Cycle of Execution
   Regardless of the nature of the business, every company needs to strengthen four main functions:

   1. Marketing
   2. Sales
   3. Operations
   4. Finance

   Marketing generates a demand for the company's products and services. This is done by bringing awareness of the kind of work or products that the company provides to prospective customers. Typically, a company advertises its offerings, educates potential customers, or otherwise engages in outreach. The goal of Marketing is to attract potential customers to the company in the form of leads.

   Sales converts leads, or prospects, into customers by providing pricing, negotiating terms of delivery, setting expectations, and securing orders. This includes repeat sales to existing customers or new sales to new customers.

   Operations delivers the product or service the customer requested in the sales process. This is where the value for the customer is generated and often describes what the company does. The primary goal of operations is to deliver the product to the customer profitably while meeting or exceeding expectations with high levels of consistency, quality, and repeatability.

Finance is responsible for monitoring and managing the resources, primarily capital, to ensure smooth functioning of the company. The main goals of Finance are to ensure that the company has enough short-term cash flow and is making the correct long-term capital allocations decisions for long-term prosperity and sustainability. Ultimately, the output of Finance is profit in the form of a return on the investment in the company.

Combined, these functions form the cycle of execution of the company. Marketing generates demand; Sales converts demand into orders; Operations delivers orders; and Finance manages resources so that the cycle can continue anew (See Figure 5.1).

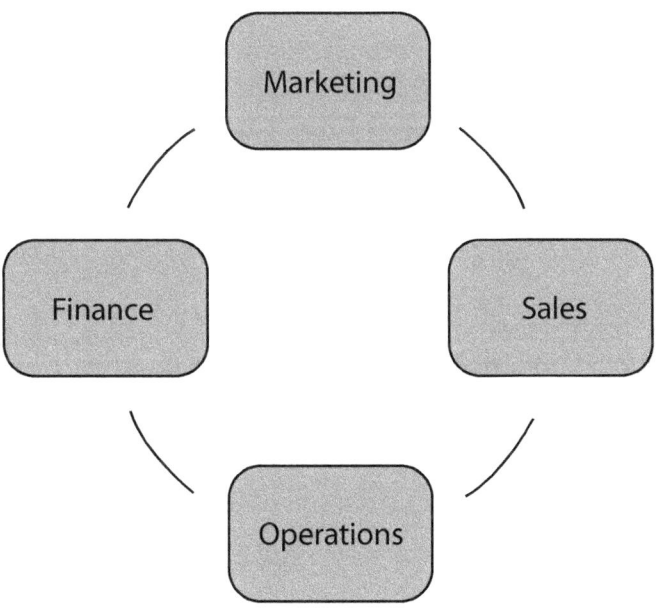

Figure 5.1: The Cycle of Execution

As a company matures, the boundaries between these functions blend into each other and instead of distinct functions they converge to become the four strands of the braid of execution. As in any rope, all strands of the rope must be equally strong for the overall rope to be strong. If any single strand is weak, the entire rope is weakened. Furthermore, because each of these functions feeds into the other, the capacity of the weakest function will serve as the overarching constraint for the whole company. For example, let's say a company's Operations can create twenty widgets a month and its Marketing can generate demand for fifteen widgets. If its Sales can only generate orders for ten widgets, guess how many widgets the company will sell? That's right, ten! It doesn't matter how good each function is individually; they have to work together as a system and that's what determines the overall output or profit. That brings us to the first exercise that the team does during Intensity Day, the System of Work audit.

2. System of Work Audit

   This is a powerful tool and process that every leadership team can use to identify the constraints in the business. The first step is to layout the four functions as steps in a process flow from left to right (See Figure 5.2).

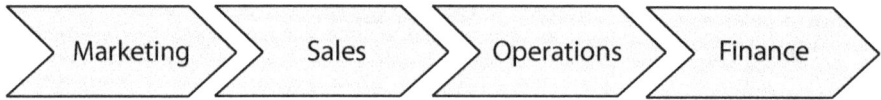

Figure 5.2: The Flow of Work

As you can see, the output of Marketing flows into Sales, Sales leads to Operations, and Operations feeds Finance, which then feeds back into Marketing, etc. Thinking about the business this way enables us to start identifying the important aspects of each of the steps for each function as follows:

1. Input or Drivers

2. Desired Output

3. Current Capacity

4. Processes

5. Tools and Resources

6. Functions

7. Time in System

8. Variability

9. Internal Constraints

10. External Constraints

Inputs or Drivers are the work or initiative that comes into each step. In the case of Marketing, since this is the start of the flow, the marketing plan outlines the campaigns that can be supported by the capital available, which is the input. In the case of Sales, the inputs are the leads that are generated by Marketing. For Operations, the inputs are the orders generated by Sales, and for Finance, the inputs are the value generated by Operations. Ultimately, the output of Finance is profit in the form of a return on the investment in the company. The profit is then reinvested back into Marketing for the cycle to continue.

Desired Outputs are the outcomes or work produced by each step. As we saw in the earlier paragraph, the output of each step is the input of the following step.

Current Capacity informs us as to the amount of work that each step can produce in a given amount of time. Another term for this is throughput. This is important to know for each step as it is the first step in understanding flow. For example, let's say that Marketing produces a large number of leads that Sales converts to orders. If Operations can only handle half the number of orders, we will soon see work accumulating between Sales and Operations, resulting in unhappy customers. It also follows that the throughput of the entire organization will be constrained by the smallest capacity of the all the steps. One advantage of laying out the flow of work this way is that leaders can immediately pinpoint a challenge that most growing companies have: Is it a marketing or sales issue? Many companies mistake a marketing problem (not attracting enough prospects) with sales (successfully converting leads into paying customers) and throw sales people at the problem, asking them to make cold calls, a marketing activity. Not only is this costly, but it results in low morale. Most good sales people don't like making cold calls, and it is often a waste of good talent when companies make them do this.

Processes are the repeatable methods used by each person responsible for the steps in the flow needed to produce the work. The best processes consistently produce high-quality work while using resources efficiently. Process design is a trade-off that depends on what you want to emphasize. A process that emphasizes quality over cost will look a lot different than one that emphasizes cost over quality. For example, the process of boarding passengers for a flight could actually be very simple. However, the need to maximize security requires that we need to carry the proper identification and become quick-change artists when it comes to footwear and other clothing accessories that have the potential of scaring jumpy detection equipment and security personnel. This makes the process quite a bit more cumbersome for passengers. Whether it's beneficial and actually improves security is left as an exercise for the reader to determine.

Tools and Resources are used by *Processes* to accomplish work. These are a combination of infrastructure and support. For example, tools might be manufacturing equipment and software, whereas resources might include capital and internal and external services.

Functions are the specific roles played by team members who carry out the *Processes* using *Tools and Resources*. For example, in a kitchen there may be a head, or executive, chef who is responsible for creating the menu and managing all activities in the kitchen. In icube™, we call this a function. Under this function we often have another function called the *sous* chef (*sous* means "under" in French), who is the second in command and the leader of the kitchen in the absence of the head chef. As we will see later, all the different functions that we identify in the team make up the Functional Framework.

Time in System identifies how much time is taken for work to be completed from Input to Output. The longer *Time in System* a job requires, the greater the capital and resource requirements, and all else equal, the greater the cost of the final product. This is why cheese that is aged longer is usually more expensive than younger cheeses.

Variability deals with reducing variations in the steps of a process so as to increase consistency. Variability can pertain to time, quality, or even quantity of the work. Effective systems need to minimize variability since it can cause bottlenecks and disruption. High variability can also reduce overall throughput even if average throughput is high. The intuitive way to understand variability is to imagine what happens when traffic doesn't flow smoothly on the expressway. If Driver A slows down, this causes Driver B to hit the brakes, thus causing Driver C to slow down, etc. In other words, we now have a chain reaction. If, however, Driver A speeds up, this leaves a gap between Driver A and Driver B that causes Driver B to speed up, making the traffic move in fits and starts. This traffic pattern demonstrates high variability. With low variability, everyone drives at the same speed, the traffic flow is even and uniform, and the overall throughput, the number of cars moving on the expressway, is high. Usually variability occurs when the type of work that is being done isn't consistent. A simple example of variability in a business would be the experience of a stylist at a hair salon. The amount of time it takes to give haircuts could vary substantially from client to client depending on needs and desired results. Similarly, if there isn't a defined process or method, different stylists will take different amounts of time to do the same work.

Internal Constraints are the factors that affect throughput or process flow that are within the control of the team. These can usually be addressed by deploying capital or reworking configurations. For example, an internal constraint could be the capacity of the manufacturing equipment that is used to produce a widget. It might be easy to increase capacity by purchasing additional equipment or reconfiguring the existing equipment.

External Constraints, on the other hand, are factors are out of the control of the team and are usually not addressable by deploying additional capital. For example, an external constraint might be imposed because of licensing restrictions. Another type of external constraint might the limitations of what is scientifically possible. As one scientist mentioned to me, "It's not a good idea to argue with physics!"

With all of these factors in mind, the facilitator guides the team through the System of Work Audit. It's important to note that this is the time to focus on the status of the current work system, not to solve any actual issues. That comes later. To accomplish this, the facilitator uses the System of Work Audit table. (See Table 5.1).

	Marketing	Sales	Operations	Finance
Input				
Output				
Capacity				
Processes				
Tools and Resources				
Functions				
Time				
Variability				
Internal Constraints				
External Constraints				

Table 5.1: System of Work Audit

Now the facilitator guides the team through the exercise starting with Marketing followed by each of the other steps. Since this is the first group exercise, the facilitator needs to be extra vigilant to ensure that the ground rules and other norms are set right from the start. Any bad habits or unproductive dynamics must be nipped in the bud. The facilitator must also pay close attention to be sure the conversation doesn't get derailed. He or she should use the Issues List to record areas of disagreement or topics that require further analysis so that the exercise stays on track and all questions are clearly recorded. Examples of issues that arise during this activity include the following: a) What is the desired output? b) How should we compute capacity? c) Do we have three processes or four? d) Is the variability in a step high or low? The facilitator uses his or her judgment to determine how much time to allocate for discussion of such questions. If the team comes to a quick conclusion, then it is recorded on the board; otherwise, the question is added to the issues list and the conversation moves to the next topic.

3. Prioritization

    The last item in the exercise is to rank the System of Work that need the most attention from an urgency and importance standpoint. Sometimes a particular functional area such as Marketing or Sales may stand out as a bottleneck. The team needs to decide whether this is something it can accomplish in ninety days or if it requires a longer timeframe. If it is the former, fixing the bottleneck is listed as a quarterly Wildly Important Goal (WIG). We will look at WIGs more closely later in this chapter.

    In my experience, most business owners often believe they have a Sales or Finance problem. Digging deeper, however, often reveals that it's Marketing and sometimes Operations that need to be fixed. Learning this about a company is a process of discovery much like trying to carve out a path across a thick forest. Having a great set of numbers, as we will see later on, is the machete that the leadership team uses to clear out the thickets.

    Upon the completion of this exercise, the facilitator announces the first to-do of the day's session: Documenting the System of Work Audit. The facilitator invites a volunteer to complete this task before the first tactical meeting following the Intensity Day. At this point, the facilitator should ask the team if they wish to take a short break.

Team

Having looked at the System of Work, we now look at the next element of Intelligence, the Team. The tool we use to accomplish this is called the Functional Framework. An effective Functional Framework enables a company to clearly handle the complexity that naturally occurs when a team grows by identifying the specific functions or roles people play in the System of Work and streamlining communications.

1. Complexity

    Complexity can occur when there is a lack of clarity as a team grows. Furthermore, as we discussed in Chapter 3, complexity grows geometrically in proportion to team size as we can see below:

- When you have a team of two people, A and B, there is just one conversation: AB.

- When you have a team of three people, A, B, and C there are three conversations: AB, BC, and CA.

- With a team of four people, A, B, C, and D, there are six conversations: AB, BC, CD, AC, AD, and BD

- A team of twenty people can have a potential of 190 conversations!

If there is any miscommunication or misunderstanding in terms of roles, responsibilities, process definition, or priorities, these conversations will ultimately result in confusion. Since value is created when team members collaborate effectively, having these conversations is critical to create a thriving organization. Having a Functional Framework with clearly defined functions and responsibilities brings forth the clarity, raises the value of these individual conversations, and ensures that all the collaboration is aligned with the goals and objectives of the company. It's important to note here that I see complexity as a relative concept. What is complex to me may be simple to someone else. Please refer to Chapter 3 for a deeper discussion on how I view the notion of complexity and its sources.

2. The icube™ Functional Framework

    In Chapter 1, we looked at how companies typically grow. When this happens, the organization chart looks like Figure 1.1. We also saw the problems this causes and how the "boss" becomes the bottleneck for information flow and decision making. Now let's look at how a company can recraft itself to avoid this problem using a Functional Framework. The icube™ Functional Framework accomplishes several objectives:

    1. It encompasses all the major functions: Marketing, Sales, Operations, and Finance into one a holistic structure.

    2. It establishes clear lines of communication without sacrificing the organic, "watercooler" talk in a company.

    3. It enables the leadership team and other teams within the organization to maximize throughput and profit and easily spot deficiencies and bottlenecks.

4. It establishes a team-based mindset across the whole company. A team-based mindset moves away from the notion of one "boss" calling all the shots to a group that seeks out the expertise and opinions of each team member and incorporates that input into all major decisions. This helps avoid one person having all and/or too much power, which, in turn, helps that one person from experiencing burn out from trying to do too much. This does not, however, mean that there has to be consensus. Every team has to have a single leader; however, the leader solicits the opinions of all team members and then makes the decision that is best for the team. My experience with teams is that this approach is far more effective and satisfying for team members, as well as for leaders.

5. It sets up the organization for successful execution by clearly defining teams that participate in tactical and strategic meetings.

With this background, let's look at the basic icube™ Functional Framework (See Figure 5.3).

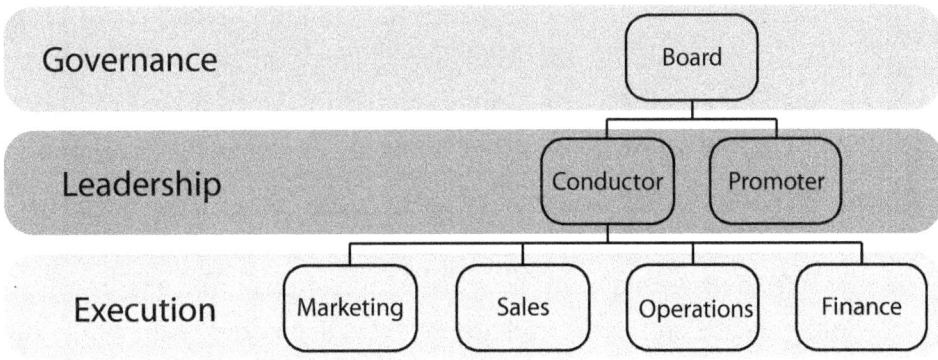

Figure 5.3: The icube™ Functional Framework

As you can see, the foundation of the icube™ Functional Framework is the Execution layer. This comprises each of the four functions that we identified earlier: Marketing, Sales, Operations, and Finance. Each of these boxes represents a role that has one leader who is accountable for executing the corresponding System of Work. While these are the simplest depictions, in reality it is possible that a function may be split up into other specific functions more appropriate for the business. For example, a wholesale distributor may split up its Operations function into Warehouse and Delivery with the former function being primarily responsible for tasks such as inventory management, picking, stocking, etc. and the latter for staging orders, routing, and delivery. Similarly, the Sales function could be split up into channel sales and direct sales. The important thing is to ensure that the Functional Framework can support the System of Work that were defined in the earlier part of the session.

In addition, it's also important to note that each of these functions may have other functions accountable to it. Continuing with the examples above, the Warehouse function may have Purchasing and Floor Management under it, while Delivery could have Order Management and Shipping under it. In larger organizations, there could be additional functional layers as needed.

Above the Execution layer is the Leadership layer. The two main functions here are the Conductor and Promoter. These functions form the core of the leadership team and are pivotal to the ongoing success of the company. Each of these functions should be assigned to a leader in the organization who is best suited for it. Not doing so can result in frustration. In some teams, the founder realizes that he or she is best suited to take on a task that is closely related to the technical or operational elements of the business rather than the Conductor or Promoter. In such situations, the Functional Framework process helps uncover this and allows the founder to step out of a function that he or she doesn't love to do. We shall see below in the section on responsibilities that some people make great Conductors and others great Promoters. And while there are a few individuals who can be good at both functions, these are few and far between.

The other point to note is that for companies in slow-moving industries, the Promoter role is optional but the Conductor role is essential. However, for companies that are in industries experiencing rapid or quantum changes, driven by new business models or technologies, both roles are absolutely critical for long-term sustainable growth and prosperity. Companies that have the right leaders in each of these functions are the most fortunate and often demonstrate an uncanny ability to grow and generate value. An excellent example of the magic of this kind of partnership is that of Steve Jobs (Promoter) and Tim Cook (Conductor) at Apple Computer. During this time, the company introduced products such as the iPod, the iTunes music store, the iPad, and the iPhone to name a few. That is not to say, however, that Cook himself hasn't done an incredible job of leading the company playing the dual role of Promoter and Conductor since the passing of Jobs in 2011 and as of this writing.

Finally, at the top of the Functional Framework is the board. This is actually a team that is responsible for the governance of the company and its long-term sustainability and viability.

Responsibilities

With the basic structure in place, let's take a look at some of the responsibilities that each of these functions has. Please note that these are the core suggestions from an icube™ perspective. Your company might have some specific circumstances and needs that would be reflected in addition to the responsibilities outlined here:

1. Board
   The board is primarily responsible for the long-term direction and purpose for a business. The four main responsibilities of the board are as follows:

   - Establishing and monitoring the culture

   - Leading the vision and mission

   - Providing strategic guidance

   - Maintaining the brand focus (Described in detail in Chapter 7)

   As you see from the Functional Framework, the board influences the organization through the Promoter and Conductor. In effect, it should guide strategy but not interfere in execution. Typically, a board is made up of individuals elected by the owners of the business. Many small businesses don't have formal boards. The concept here is to introduce "board thinking" into the mix. For companies that do, the selection of members is both an art and a science. Effective boards are teams in their own right and must be able to carry out the duties described above to benefit the company. They must be able to guide the strategy and have the discipline to not interfere. A good guideline is that board members should have a "noses in, fingers out" policy. They should know what's going on and ensure that any concerns are addressed by using the Functional Framework as the guide to communicating this to the leadership of the team. Note to the reader: Constructing effective boards is a big topic outside the scope of this book. I have briefly touched upon it in Chapter 10, and it is potential material for the *Advanced icube™ Concepts* book.

2. Promoter
   The Promoter is usually someone with big ideas and vision. The Promoter has the following responsibilities:

   - External facing elements of Intelligence (Customer, Value Proposition, and Product or Service definition)
   - Big relationships
   - Big ideas
   - Guiding the brand linkage (Described in detail in Chapter 7)

   The Promoter works closely with the Conductor as a co-strategist along with the board for guidance.

3. Conductor
   Much like the conductor of an orchestra, the Conductor is ultimately responsible for managing the flow of work in the organization and overseeing the execution functions. The primary responsibilities of this function are:

   - Internal facing elements of Intelligence (Team, System of Work, and Numbers)
   - Constraint identification and flow management
   - Issue resolution in meetings
   - Monitoring of brand alignment (Described in detail in Chapter 7)

As you might guess, the Conductor serves as a buffer and balances the energy and enthusiasm of the Promoter. While a Promoter churns out idea after idea, the Conductor focuses on stability, throughput, and quality. When these functions work well together, a company can generate immense value and profit. Now that we know the responsibilities of the leadership roles, we can look at the responsibilities of each of the execution functions.

4. Marketing

The main goal of marketing is customer attraction in the form of leads. The marketing department is like the flower on a plant whose primary objective is to attract bees to help it pollinate. The main responsibilities are:

- Define, execute, and measure the System of Work
- Define and execute strategy and tactics
- Ensure that the brand management is aligned with the strategy of the entire organization

As seen above, a successful Marketing function interfaces with Sales, which we will review next.

5. Sales

The primary task of Sales is to convert leads and customer interest into commitments or orders. Its core responsibilities are:

- Define, execute, and measure the System of Work
- Validate customer needs
- Lead the process of establishing pricing

Sales has direct contact with prospects and customers and as such has the best information on how to affect a transaction. That does not mean that Sales decides pricing; instead it means that this function has the best knowledge with which to enable the leadership team to make these decisions.

6. Operations

Operations is the function that delivers value to the customer.

This is where the work gets done. The main responsibilities of Operations are:

- Define, execute, and measure the System of Work
- Execute value delivery
- Lead the process of establishing costs

Here as well it is important to note that Operations knows best what it takes to do the work that delivers value to customers. Hence, it provides cost information to the rest of the leadership team who uses it to make decisions about product or service definition, configuration, packaging, quality, etc., all of which can impact cost.

7. Finance

    Finance manages the money in the company. In the process of doing this, it needs to carry out the following responsibilities:

    - Define, execute, and measure the System of Work
    - Manage day-to-day cash flow
    - Manage long-term capital allocation in accordance with the direction of the company

Finance needs to work with all the other functions to ensure that it has a handle on the profitability of the company and the cash flow cycle. This function also needs to guide the rest of the leadership team in providing input on decisions related to new investment such as expansions and capital expenditures.

 At this point, the facilitator guides the leadership team to define the Functional Framework for their business. Typically, the team will start referring to functions by the names of the people that they think are performing them. For example, they might say, "Diana, you're the Promoter" or "Raj, you're the Conductor." The facilitator should gently discourage this behavior and start pointing out that the objective in building the Functional Framework is to put the structure in place from a functional standpoint and that assignments to these functions will be made later. The facilitator does this by focusing on the specific functions, the responsibilities of that function, and how that function relates to the others, effectively making up the Functional Framework.

Often a company may not have recognized the need for some of the functions identified here. Instead, they may have an organizational chart that doesn't clearly identify functions and responsibilities. That's when the facilitator could use Figure 5.3 as a starting point and for each function ask if the function in question is appropriate for this team. A Functional Framework discussion can take some time. Invariably, the first cut isn't the correct one. That's okay. However, it's a good idea for the team to have something in place that they all agree to test for a period of ninety days until the first quarterly strategic review. Once the team has decided on a Functional Framework, they can then move to the next step in this process, which is assignments.

Assignments

Now the team is ready to begin assigning names to functions. The process we follow in icube™ is based on the approach described by Jim Collins in his book, *Good to Great*. Collins describes a company as being like a bus. First, you need to get the right people on the bus, and after that you need to decide which seat each individual should occupy. A "right person" is someone who embodies all the core values of the business. At this stage, we have not yet defined the core values of the business, at least not in icube™. So our focus is the Right Seat.

To determine the right seat for a person, we use another concept also introduced by Collins called the *Hedgehog Review*. A hedgehog excels at one task while a fox is good at many and doesn't excel at anything in particular. In a team, if we have everyone who is performing a function passing the *Hedgehog Review*, we will have a very strong team. The *Hedgehog Review* is carried out by asking three simple questions:

- Does the person love carrying out most all the responsibilities of the function?
- Is the person great at executing the function?

- Does the person add economic value to the organization by executing the function?

If the answer to all three questions is *yes*, then the person is in the right seat for that function. With this in mind, the facilitator guides the team to focus on the *Right Seat* aspect when making assignments for the Functional Framework. With these as well, it is important to note that the team is implicitly agreeing to put assignments in place for the next ninety days until the next quarterly review. As a team puts the Functional Framework in place, it may see gaps in the leadership team in that there isn't really a best fit for a particular function. This is natural and to be expected. The fix for this is to assign someone from the team on a temporary basis and to add this gap as an issue to the Issues List. When this happens, you may see the same name assigned to multiple functions on the Functional Framework. Over time, however, as the team grows, the Functional Framework matures to the point where each team member is assigned a single function.

The other point to make here is that as we proceed further down the functions in the company, it's possible that there are multiple people assigned to the same function. Those functions are represented either as multiple boxes on the Functional Framework or clearly indicated in some other fashion. It is critical that the Functional Framework be easy to understand and not overly complicated.

As mentioned earlier, the *Right Person* assessment is actually made during the quarterly review. This is done within an exercise called the *Trust Review*. It's a good idea at this time for the facilitator to introduce the *Trust Review* to familiarize the team with the process.

3. Trust Review

    The *Trust Review* is a deceptively simple, yet powerful exercise that can increase team cohesiveness and bring up difficult issues related to interpersonal dynamics in a safe and respectful way. Ultimately, its objective is to enhance the communication within the team, the lack of which is often at the root of most problems related to team dynamics. There are two components of the *Trust Review*:

1. 360 Feedback

2. Personal Report

Both of these are delivered candidly in person in front of the whole team. First, a team member receives feedback. Then, that same team member gives his or her feedback to the rest of the group. It is critical that the facilitator, leaders in a position of power, and team members all work together to ensure that the environment remain open, honest, respectful, and safe. Specifically, anything said during a *Trust Review* should always be treated fairly and reviewed objectively. In my experience, whenever a leader demonstrates the ability to absorb critical feedback without taking it personally and truly makes an effort to understand and assimilate it, this behavior can radically improve the trust and cohesiveness of the team, and others will follow suit. On the contrary, when leaders demonstrate a thin skin and the inability to take critical feedback, this sets the stage for others to shut down and renders the exercise meaningless. Here the facilitator has to have his or her spider-sense at full power and pay attention to the dynamics in the room. Depending on what's going on, the facilitator may decide that the team isn't ready for a full-fledged *Trust Review*.

With that in mind, let's look at how to conduct a *Trust Review*. The process starts by having one person in the team be the subject. The facilitator may ask for volunteers or simply choose an order like starting with the person on the left or right at the table. After a subject is selected, the two components are conducted:

1. 360 Feedback

    In 360 Feedback, each team members provides feedback to the subject of the review on the following elements:

    Right Person
    As we saw earlier, the *Right Person* is someone who embodies all the core values of the organization. The core values are articulated during the vision-building workshop described in detail in Chapter 7 and will have been completed before the first quarterly review. The facilitator records any issues relative to this part.

Right Seat

Right Seat assessments are made using the *Hedgehog Review* described earlier during the assignments portion of the Functional Framework discussion. Here also the facilitator makes note of any issues that might be brought up.

Blind Spots

The blind spot feedback is based on a very powerful tool called the *Johari Window* developed by the psychologists Joseph Luft and Harrington Ingham (Luft & Ingham, 1955). "The Johari window [is] a graphic model of interpersonal awareness." This tool was designed to uncover blind spots and is actually quite simple (See Figure 5.4).

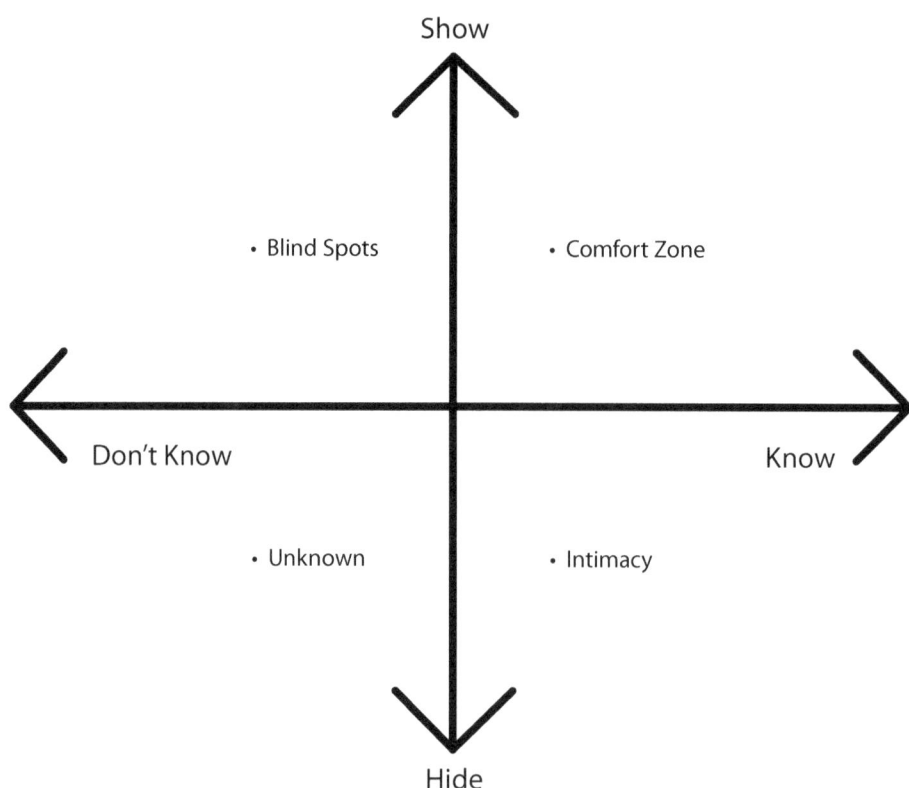

Figure 5.4: Johari Window Blindspots

We all have traits we know of and show others. We also have traits we know of but hide from others. Some traits are unknown to us and not observable by others. Finally, there are traits that we show others but are unaware of ourselves.

Let's look at the right side of the figure. The "Know/Show" quadrant is our comfort zone. These are the behaviors and habits we are comfortable sharing with people we don't know too well or even strangers. Then as we get to know someone, if we feel more comfortable in the relationship and as trust builds, we go into the "Know/Hide" quadrant with that person. This means we start sharing with that person the traits that we usually hide from others. We tend to do this as we start building trust and increase intimacy with a person. On the left side of the figure are the traits that are unknown to us. Those that are in our "Don't know/Hide" are behaviors or drivers that are both unknown to us and others. There's not much we can do about these as we go through life experiences, but increased self-awareness can sometimes draw these out.

Blind spots, on the other hand, are in the "Don't know/Show" quadrant. These are behaviors that we are unaware of but others can observe. Being able to learn about blind spots in a safe, non-judgmental setting can be hugely valuable for us as individuals and an excellent opportunity for personal growth and awareness.

Experiencing this in a team setting can bring about even more insight. As you might guess, this process can also be a bit intimidating. If there isn't a sufficient level of trust already within the team, it may be best to skip this until the quarterly review. There are no hard and fast rules on how to make this decision, and the facilitator needs to make the call based on everything that is known about the team. After the last person has provided feedback on blind spots, the facilitator invites the subject to give the rest of the team his or her *Personal Report*.

2. Personal Report

The Personal Report wraps up the discussion for the subject. There are two main elements in the Personal Report:

1. Comments and Insights

2. Autonomy, Mastery and Purpose

1. Comments and Insights
   First, the subject shares any thoughts or insights gleaned from the feedback given by the rest of the team. This is also an opportunity for the subject to express appreciation for the effort and care demonstrated by the rest of the team during the feedback.

2. Autonomy, Mastery, and Purpose
   Following the comments, the subject then proceeds to convey to the rest of the team his or her own personal experience of working in the company and in a particular function. Specifically, in icube™, we encourage team members to articulate whether or not they have sufficient autonomy, if they believe that they are on the path to mastery, and finally, if they feel like they are part of a bigger purpose. This is based on the work done by Daniel Pink as described in his book, *Drive: The Surprising Truth About What Motivates Us*. To summarize, Pink states that beyond a base level of financial compensation, more money doesn't motivate individuals to excel at their jobs. Instead, people shine when they have sufficient autonomy, are on the path to mastery, and feel that they are part of a bigger purpose.

   The *Trust Review* concludes when all the team members have had an opportunity to be the subject, and the facilitator has noted all the issues pertaining to particular team members that arose during the process.

   Having completed the *Functional Framework*, taken a stab at assignments, and described the *Trust Review* process, the facilitator announces the second to-do of the day: Drafting the Functional Framework.

Typically, by this time, depending on the flow of the session, the team should be ready for a lunch break. Many teams are gung ho and want to keep going, but it's a good idea to take some down time before continuing with the afternoon session. This helps maintain the energy level of participants who might overestimate their abilities amid their enthusiasm!

Intensity Day Part 2: Afternoon

After a refreshing break the facilitator should assemble the team again. Let's review the progress so far. The team has completed two of the internal facing elements of Intelligence: the System of Work Audit and the Functional Framework. Then they start the afternoon session of Intensity day with the last internal facing element of Intelligence.

Numbers

The Numbers part of Intensity Day has two parts:

1. Concepts

2. Scorecard

   1. Concepts
      Having completed the System of Work Audit and the Functional Framework, the team is now ready to tackle the final component of the internal facing elements of Intelligence. Numbers provide the objective measures that take away emotion from the decision-making process. Numbers also give the team the ability to identify controllable (internal) actions and uncontrollable (external) conditions. In doing so, a team can use the numbers as a lever with which to control performance. The most effective numbers are the ones that can be controlled and result in tangible business benefit.

      As we saw earlier, when we laid out the four main foundational functions of an organization, Marketing, Sales, Operations, and Finance as steps in a process flow, we also noted that the output of one serves as the input to the following step. In this portion of the session, we attempt to put in place the measurements of these inputs and outputs. To do that, let's take a look at the broad categories of these measures (See Figure 5.5).

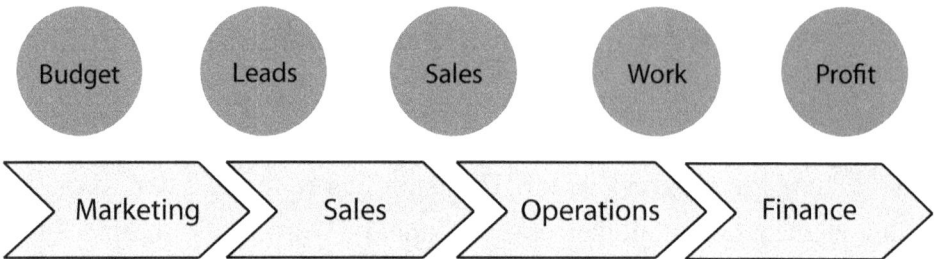

Figure 5.5: Number Categories

Business owners know that their companies need to make a healthy profit. With this in mind and working our way backwards from right to left, the category of measurement for the output of Finance is Profit. We will see later some examples of what some specific measurements might be in this category and the others listed here. The category of measurement for Operations is work done for customers. That of Sales is some measure of sales orders or contracts. Finally, Marketing is measured using a general category of leads. The input into Marketing is the capital available with some measure of budget, which is the profit that is reinvested in the business. With that in mind, the team needs to understand the following concepts as they apply to numbers: Outputs (results we want to maximize), Inputs (materials, information, or resources), Activities (controllable actions), and Influencers (uncontrollable conditions).

Outputs, Inputs, Activities, and Influencers
Outputs are the measure we want to improve. However, by the time an output is measured, it's too late to make a change. That's why outputs are *lagging* measures. The three types of numbers called *leading* measures that help us measure the impact of Outputs are:

- *Inputs*: materials, information, or resources available.
- *Activities*: controllable actions the team can execute and measure.
- *Influencers*: external conditions we can't control but need to know as they might impact activities and outputs.

For example, if you want to manage your weight, the Output is your current weight. By the time you step on the scale, it is too late to do anything about it. In other words, weight is a lagging measure. You need to know what to measure in advance of measuring weight. To do so we need to take a look at the leading measures. Inputs might be the number of hours you have available to exercise and the dollars you have to spend on personal fitness, nutrition instruction, a gym membership, healthy food purchases, etc. Activities include controllable actions such as calories consumed between weight measurements, while the measures for exercise could be number of miles walked, biked, or run or hours spent in the gym. Influencers might be measures related to the genetic metabolic profile of the individual or how he or she responds to certain diet and exercise. An Influencer might also be the outside temperature that could impact whether or not the exercise is outdoors or indoors.

As you can see in the example, just measuring the number of hours spent in the gym may not be a good measure, especially if those hours are spent chatting with other gym members! We need to measure the actual hours exercised, i.e., the actual part of the activity that makes a difference. In a business context that might be translated into measuring time spent in helping customers solve a problem (a good measure) versus measuring time spent on the phone (a poor measure).

This also shows that while outputs, or lagging measures, are usually easy to determine because most of the time we can clearly see results, leading measures such are Inputs, Activities, and Influencers are often not that straightforward and need some thoughtful consideration. However, since we have laid out the cycle of execution horizontally, our task of determining meaningful numbers is made a little simpler.

The input into Marketing is capital. Marketing is measured by leads. Sales is measured by sales orders or contracts. Operations is measured by work done for customers. Finance is measured by profit. Finally, profit is reinvested back into marketing, as well as other areas of the business.

Each step (marketing, sales, operations, and finance) is like a sub-system that generates outputs using inputs that are acted on, controllable activities that can affect the outputs, and uncontrollable influencers that can also affect the outputs.

Having a clear understanding of all the important numbers in each of these types and making it a practice to measure them can provide the leadership team the situational awareness and discipline required to run the business. A well-crafted scorecard is like the dashboard of a high-performance car in an auto race, providing the driver the critical information required to drive the vehicle with precision.

Now that we know the broad types of Inputs and Outputs for each of these steps, let's take a look at what might make up the Influencers and Activities. The team can use these to measure each step, thus resulting in an effective scorecard.

Marketing

> *Input* > profit/budget
> > *Activities*: advertising, communications, etc.
> > *Influencers*: customer response
> > > *Output* > leads

Starting from the left, the input to Marketing is the marketing budget or capital available to spend on marketing. The activities that we can control include newsletters, advertising, attendance at trade-shows, etc. The influencers that we cannot control are customer behavior and response to the activities, market trends, etc. The result that we want is a sufficiently large number of leads. Next, we move on to Sales.

Sales

> *Input* > leads
> > *Activities:* sales team response to leads
> > *Influencers*: budget cycle, customer response, etc.
> > > *Output* > orders/contracts

Continuing, the input to Sales is the leads generated by marketing. The activities that we can control are how quickly and effectively the sale team responds to and engages with incoming leads. The influencer may be the budget cycle or response of the customer. The result that we want is sales orders or contracts for services. Next, we move on to Operations.

Operations

    Input > orders/contracts
        Activities: quality checks, communication, etc.
        Influencers: actions of suppliers, customers, etc.
            Output > delivery of product/services

Similarly, the input to Operations is sales orders or contracts for services generated by Sales. Other inputs are measures such as inventory, personnel capacity, etc. The activities would be practices such as quality checks, proactive communication with customers and suppliers, having a well-trained staff, implementing safety protocols, and regular maintenance of capital equipment. Influencers may be the actions of customers, the actions of third-party service providers such as delivery companies or supplier considerations. The result or output of operations is delivery of products or services with a high level of safety, quality, accuracy, and customer satisfaction. And finally, we move on to Finance.

Finance

    Input > delivery of products/services
        Activities: communication with customers, suppliers, etc.
        Influencers: actions of lenders, customers, investors, etc.
            Output > profit

The input to Finance is the successful delivery of products and services to customers. The activities are effective and proactive outreach and communication with customers and suppliers. Sometimes, companies raise capital from external sources such as equity investors (owners in the company) or banks (lenders to the company). In such cases, the influencers are the behaviors and actions of these parties. The influencers may also be customer behavior in the form of the time it takes for them to make payments and that of suppliers in the form of terms offered for purchases. The result or output of Finance is sufficient cash flow and return on invested capital so that it can either be reinvested in the business or returned to shareholders. In the end, the cash result of Finance is the same cash input that flows back into Marketing, thus continuing the cycle.

Measures Under Test
Sometimes a team might want to know if a certain measure, usually an influencer, is useful. In such cases, the team might confer a status of "measure under test" to it and record it for a period of one or more quarters. At some point, after sufficient information is captured, the team can decide whether to retain or discard the measure. This is a good way to create a learning process within the organization.

Owner
Every measure that is selected for use must have one owner. This is the function on the Functional Framework. Having an assigned person ensures that the measure is carried out, and in case it's an activity, recorded, and reported on the scorecard.

Validation
Finally, every measure selected should be periodically (usually quarterly or annually) validated for suitability and decision-making value. Measures that are not providing any meaningful benefit should be removed from the scorecard, and if appropriate, replaced by ones that are more meaningful.

2. Scorecard

   Now the team can use these concepts to craft a scorecard that they can monitor regularly to know if the business is on track. Similar to the dashboard of a car, the scorecard is the collection of numbers the leadership team needs to run the business. A good scorecard is a combination of Outputs, Inputs, Activities, and Influencers. The Outputs and Inputs inform the team whether or not they are achieving their goals. Measuring Activities brings visibility to the actual execution, and measuring Influencers provides the team vital information on the environment so that they can adjust controllable actions as needed. Much like driving a car, the team can use the scorecard information to press on the gas pedal, ease up on it, or tap the brakes if necessary. The idea here is to put the old adage, "What is measured is improved," into practice. Refer to Table 5.2 for examples of measures that might apply to your company.

Marketing	Sales	Operations	Finance
Budget (Input)	Leads (Input)	Orders/Inventory (Inputs)	Gross Profit (Input)
Outreach (Activity)	Demos/Quotes (Activities)	Quality Control (Activity)	Collections (Activities)
Views (Influencers)	Customer Budget (Influencers)	Supplier Lead Times (Influencers)	Capital Cost (Influencers)
Leads (Output)	Orders (Output)	Gross Profit (Output)	Cash Flow/Return on Capital (Outputs)

Table 5.2: Examples of Measures

Remember that these are just examples. Refer to Table 5.3 for a scorecard worksheet that the facilitator can use to help the team uncover their measures. As you might guess, effective scorecard construction can take several iterations. Please refer to Chapter 10 for a discussion on how to use scorecards to increase collaboration and teamwork in a company.

	Marketing	Sales	Operations	Finance
Outputs				
Inputs				
Activities				
Influencers				

Table 5.3: Scorecard Worksheet

Finally, the scorecard should be put on a spreadsheet that is accessible to the team either on a shared network drive or online using a cloud-based spreadsheet application. As with the other to-dos, the facilitator announces and assigns the third to-do: Creating the scorecard. A sample scorecard is available on the Scorecard card in the icube™ Trello templates at https://www.pcsinsight.com/resources

With a completed scorecard behind them, the team is now in the home stretch of Intensity Day. Usually by this time, the team may be feeling pretty beat up. I recommend that the facilitator offer a longer break before continuing with the final three parts of the session: Meeting Beats, Issues, and Wildly Important Goals (WIGs).

Meeting Beats

Having completed the internal elements of Intelligence, the team is now ready to implement the elements of Intensity meetings. Meeting beats set up regular intervals for the team to review and solve tactical and strategic issues. Tactical issues relate to the day-to-day execution of the work in the company. Strategic issues deal with long-term factors. Below we will review a process to help you determine whether an issue is tactical or strategic. The ultimate goal of meetings is to ensure execution, accountability, and team focus. When this happens, the levels of trust and communication increase dramatically, resulting in greater productivity and profit.

1. Tactical Meetings

    Tactical meetings are usually held weekly and have a specific agenda. The next chapter describes in detail the process and agenda of a tactical meeting. At this point, the facilitator should just introduce the concept of the tactical meeting to the team. The team also commits to setting up an ongoing tactical meeting and decides on the following:

    Name

    I encourage teams to give their meeting a unique name instead of something boring like *Weekly Status Meeting*. Giving it a unique name makes it part of the company culture and not something imposed externally.

    When

    The team should also decide on a time that works for everyone, is free of most distractions, and is not likely to get cancelled. Having a meeting first thing Monday or Friday might be a good idea as these times are usually available and not usually used for customer interactions or business events. Whatever day and time the team chooses should be recorded on a central calendar in perpetuity so that it remains sacred and cancellations are few and far between.

Where

Having a specific location for tactical meetings ensures that there is no confusion and establishes a sense of stability for the team on an ongoing basis. Tactical meetings should be onsite at the company's office in a suitable conference room with equipment similar to the location used for sessions.

Facilitator

Finally, the team should designate a facilitator to run the meeting. Some companies use a single facilitator for all meetings. In others, facilitation rotates so that all team members can pick up the skill. If at all possible, I highly recommend the latter approach since being good at meeting facilitation is an excellent skill to have and can be used in other interactions such as sub-team meetings and general meetings with customers and suppliers.

2. Strategic Meetings

   During this session, the team needs to set up the schedule and other aspects of the strategic meetings as described in the section on tactical meetings. (The detailed process and agenda for facilitating strategic meetings is described in Chapter 8). In deciding the name of the strategic meeting, I recommend using a term that reflects longer-term thinking and decision making. The duration of quarterly strategic meetings should be at least a day and potentially a two-day offsite for annual meetings for larger teams. While tactical meetings can be facilitated by internal team members, there is value in bringing in an external facilitator for strategic meetings. If this is not feasible, then it's better to have an internally facilitated strategic meeting than to not have it.

3. Meeting Groupings

   No individual team member needs to be in more than two tactical meetings on an ongoing basis if the Functional Framework is designed correctly. This is accomplished by grouping functions in a single layer with all the functions that report into that function. For example, group the Board, Conductor, and Promoter together to form the board meeting group. Group the Conductor, Promoter, Marketing, Sales, Operations, and Finance together to form the Leadership team meeting group. Let's say that the Sales function had two other functions accountable to it, Direct Sales and Channel Sales. Then Sales, Direct Sales, and Channel Sales would form the Sales team meeting group and so on.

This method of grouping minimizes the amount of time people spend in meetings, yet it maximizes the visibility, collaboration, and situational awareness of teams in the entire organization. This is further enhanced if the team decides to use a system like Trello to manage its facilitation of icube™. The leadership team can put in place a policy of visibility and transparency across the entire organization as appropriate. Please refer to Chapter 10 for a deeper discussion of this concept.

Wildly Important Goals

WIGs are a concept introduced in the book, *The 4 Disciplines of Execution: Achieving Your Wildly Important Goals,* by Sean Covey, Chris McChesney, and Jim Huling. In it, the authors stress the importance of defining wildly important goals as a clear and unambiguous objective for the team to accomplish. In icube™, we define two types of WIGs: Quarterly and Annual. Quarterly WIGs are first established during the Intensity Day session and then reviewed quarterly. Annual WIGs are established during the Vision Building Workshop as described in Chapter 7 and reviewed annually.

In this session, the team takes a stab at defining the quarterly WIGs that will be accomplished over the next ninety days. The facilitator uses all the information that has been discussed, including issues that were identified in the earlier part of the session, to guide this part of the conversation. As noted earlier, the System of Work identifies the critical constraints in the flow of the organization. Similarly, the Functional Framework discussion uncovers gaps in the team. The numbers discussion may uncover the need to measure a key metric. All of these are candidates for quarterly WIGs. As the team starts listing WIGs, the facilitator keeps in mind the following guidelines:

1. Representation

    WIGs should always be represented in the following form: Objective from X to Y (in Z days). Here, the Objective is the intended goal, X is the current value of the measurement, Y is the value we want to reach, and Z is the number of days in which to accomplish the Objective. This form of representation ensures that there is a clear understanding and agreement of whether or not the goal was reached by the next quarter. This also helps the team understand whether or not the goal is achievable in the time available with respect to the value of the measure today. Since we are setting up a quarterly WIG, the value of Z is always ninety days.

For example, let's say that the leadership team wants to increase the number of referrals from its customers to new prospects. The team has uncovered that it could do a better job with customer satisfaction, and in doing so, increase the number of referrals. They also decide that this should be a WIG and frame it with some numbers such as, "Increase customer satisfaction score from 8.1 to 9.0." This means that using some internal system that they already have in place, the customer satisfaction score that is 8.1 today needs to be raised to 9.0. In executing this WIG, the team will first need to understand the major factors leading to the low score, implement practices to address those factors, and measure customer satisfaction again before the next quarter.

In the event that a WIG doesn't pertain to making a change that is measurable, it is critical that the team ask itself whether or not their vision of what completion looks like is crystal clear. Sometimes I suggest teams put a *Doneness* checklist in the WIG that has smaller clearly defined elements, each of which can be clearly evaluated as done or not done. This way, the entire WIG is completed only if all the items on the *Doneness* checklist are done.

2. Number

    It's not at all unusual for teams to try to bite off more than they can chew. The process of laying out the business structures and processes as described earlier serves to clarify things and can uncover many areas of improvement. It is very tempting for teams to try and resolve everything that they see. However, there is a great risk in doing this. If the team decides on too many WIGs, it can overwhelm members, and this can have a detrimental impact on team morale and productivity. Instead, it is best to have a small number of wildly important goals to direct the priorities of the team. This not only increases focus but completing goals on time enhances a sense of accomplishment that can substantially improve team morale, cohesiveness, and confidence, which can then increase productivity and profit. The facilitator should guide the team to have a small number of WIGs. One is ideal, two is fine, and three is okay. Having any more than that can introduce the risks described earlier.

3. Owner
   Each WIG should be owned by a single person on the team. This doesn't mean that he or she does all the work, but he or she is ultimately accountable to the rest of the team to accomplish the WIG. The rest of the team should support the WIG owner to ensure that the WIG is completed.

   Validation
   Finally, the team should ensure that the scorecard developed earlier is aligned with each WIG. One or more activities should directly influence the WIG, and the results and predictors should be related to the WIG. This ensures that the WIG has a high chance of being completed.

Issues List Review

This is the last group exercise of the session. The objective of the Issues List review is two-fold:

1. Condensing
   Condensing is the process of combining or eliminating issues so that the list that remains is made up of unique items and no duplicates. It also ensures that multiple related issues are merged into a single issue that can more comprehensively capture all details at hand. Reducing the number of issues also makes the final list easier to manage.

2. Categorizing
   After condensing the issues into a shorter list, the facilitator guides the team to categorize the issue into tactical and strategic issues. This is accomplished using the simple time management method described in the book, *The 7 Habits of Highly Effective People: Powerful Lessons in Personal Change* by Stephen R. Covey (See Figure 5.6).

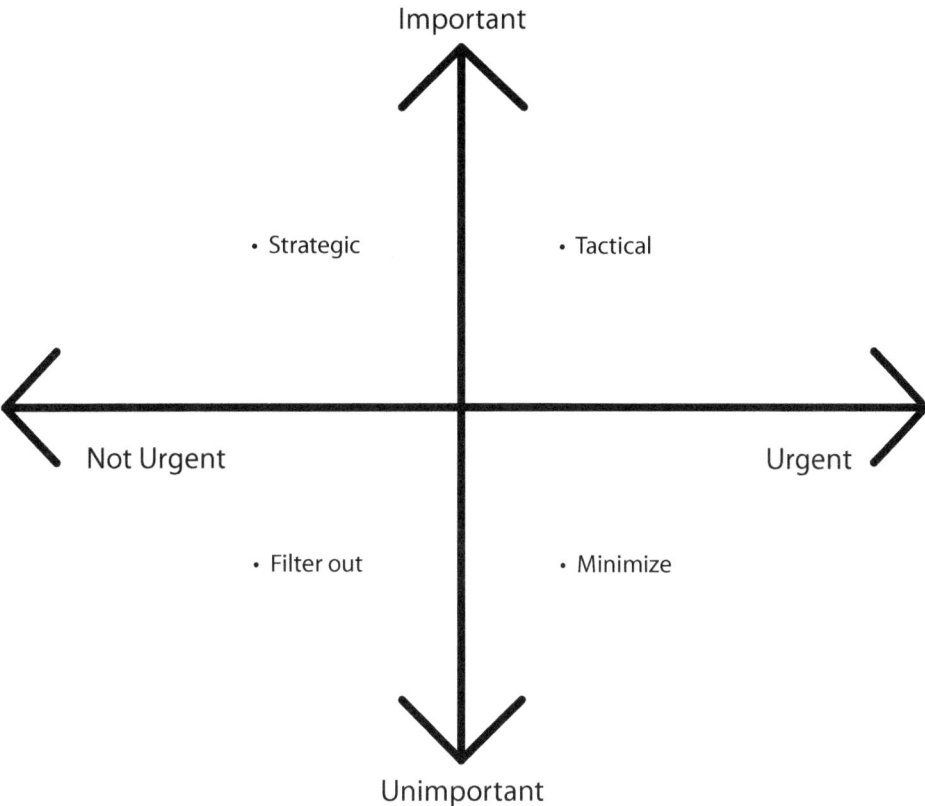

Figure 5.6: Categorizing Issues

Using Covey's method, we can put all issues in the four quadrants:

- Unimportant and Not Urgent
  These issues are actually non-issues and can be ignored.

- Unimportant and Urgent
  These issues are often a reflection of an opportunity to improve a process and should be minimized. For example, if a customer is unhappy because he or she was not informed of the date that our product would be delivered, we could communicate the customer's delivery date and record an acknowledgement using a process.

- Important and Urgent
  These are the issues the team needs to discuss and resolve in the tactical meetings.

- Important and Not Urgent
  Longer-term, big-picture strategic issues are usually tabled and reviewed during strategic reviews.

The facilitator guides the team and each remaining issue is marked with a T (Tactical) or S (Strategic). This effectively wraps up the business portion of the Intensity Day.

Trello Setup Plan

The last item of the agenda before concluding the session is to decide whether or not the team will be using Trello (www.trello.com) to manage its implementation of icube™. Unless the team has an alternative to Trello in the form of a workflow management system, notwithstanding the disclaimer earlier in this chapter, I highly recommend that they use it. The downside is minimal, the software is free to use for basic functionality and is available for a reasonable fee per user for business class features. Assuming that the team will be using Trello, the teams should accomplish the following tasks prior to the first tactical meeting following the Intensity Day session:

- ◇ Create Trello team
- ◇ Copy all the boards from https://trello.com/icubetemplates to boards within the team
- ◇ Invite team members to Trello
- ◇ Add all team members to the boards
- ◇ Prepare the Tactical Meeting board as follows:
  - Change the name of the board to reflect the meeting name decided by the team.
  - Add cards to the WIG list, select the team member that owns the WIG and add his or her name to the card, and change the label to *New/In Progress.*
  - Add to-do cards for each of the team members who have agreed to complete the System of Work Audit, Functional Framework, and Scorecard during the session. Mark each of the cards as *New/In Progress.*

- Add cards for each of the tactical issues on the list called *Issues*.
- Change the date on the *Conclude* card in the *Closing* list to reflect the date of the first tactical meeting.

◇ Prepare the Strategic Meeting board as follows:

- Change the name of the board to reflect the meeting name decided by the team.
- Copy the *Meeting Template* card to a card called *Quarterly Review YYYY/MM/DD* (date of the first quarterly review).
- Add a card for each of the strategic issues in the list called *Strategic Issues*.

The task of setting up Trello is best handled by someone from the team who is computer savvy and able to find his or her way around new software applications quickly. The nice thing about Trello is that it is very easy to get used to and most team members don't need to do a lot of heavy lifting in terms of setting up the software or using it. Team members who have volunteered for the various to-dos will see that the Trello templates available at the link mentioned above have cards that contain Microsoft®, Power Point®, and Excel® files that can be used as templates to accomplish their tasks.

Closing

The facilitator and the team can now breathe a sigh of relief that they are done! The facilitator verifies the following to wrap up the session:

◇ Are all to-dos and owners recorded?

◇ Are all the WIGs and owners recorded?

◇ Tactical issues captured?

◇ Strategic issues captured?

◇ Trello setup plan in place?

Assuming everything is in order, the facilitator may go around the room and ask each team member to provide a session rating from 1–10. The objective of this exercise is to look for any feedback particularly as it relates to low scores that can then be captured as a tactical or strategic issue as appropriate. Hopefully that doesn't happen, and instead, the team is able to conclude the session feeling tired and enthused at the same time!

Coffee Talk with Robert

As Light Craft concluded their Intensity Day session, the team marveled at the amount of work they accomplished. For the first time, they saw their company as a combination of distinct and separate, yet connected, areas, each having a specific task and leader. The Functional Framework (See Figure 5.7) finally gave them a clear structure for the business.

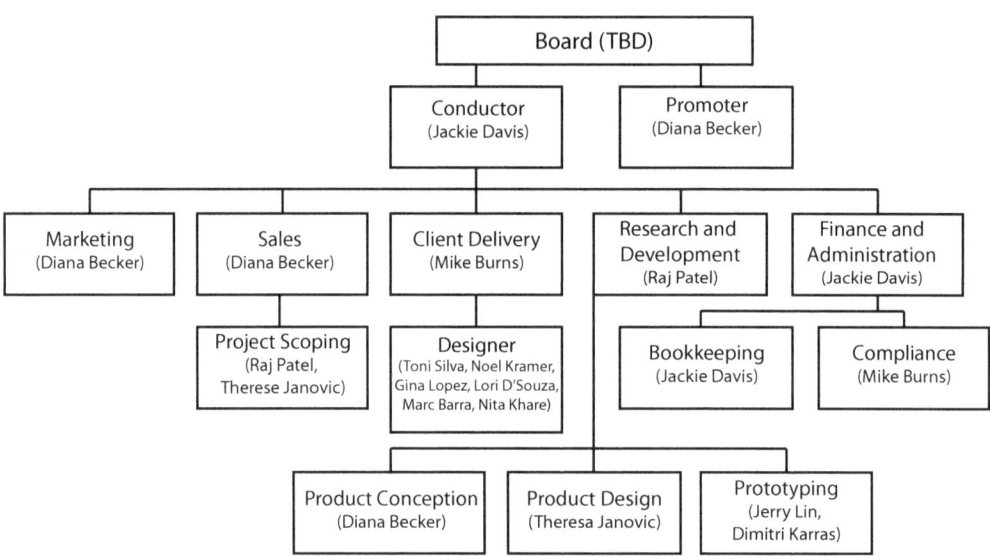

Figure 5.7: Light Craft Innovations, LLC – Functional Framework

Before Intensity Day, the team wasn't always clear if the company was on track. Yes, they could ask Diana, but often she didn't have the complete picture before Jackie was able to produce the financials, and often that was too late. The scorecard (See Table 5.4) they crafted, however, gave every team member a clear understanding of the numbers they needed to hit to keep Light Craft winning.

Measurable	Owner	Goal
New Project Leads (Output)	Diana	> 20 per month
Stakeholder/Executive Contacts (Activity)	Diana	> 1 per week
New Content Piece Developed and Distributed (Influencer)	Diana	> 1 per month
Active Quoted Dollars (Activity)	Raj	>$1.7M per month
Closed Sales (Output)	Raj	>$900K per month
Average Project Quote Time (Activity)	Raj	< 3 weeks
All Projects On Track (Output)	Mike	Yes
Average Client Satisfaction Score (Output)	Mike	> 8.5
All Active Clients/Projects Reviewed per Month (Activity)	Mike	Yes
Regional Construction Activity Index (Influencer)	Mike	N/A
Active High Value Prototype Projects (Measure Under Test)	Raj	Unknown
Days Sales Outstanding (Output)	Jackie	< 30
Working Capital (Output)	Jackie	> $1.2M
All Past Due Customers Contacted per Month (Activity)	Jackie	Yes

Table 5.4: Scorecard for Light Craft Innovations, LLC

Diana recalled that Robert was out of town at a conference and decided to send him a quick text saying that Light Craft had taken its first major step in the icube™ journey. She could tell that Robert was both delighted and probably very busy when she got back his two smiley faces and thumbs up emojis in response.

Vision Track

- ◇ How are you feeling right now?
- ◇ Are there any tactical and/or strategic issues that you have identified?
- ◇ What major issues do you see impacting the implementation of icube™ for your team?

Action Track To-Dos

- ◇ Ensure that the owner of the Functional Framework has access to all the information about it and all the tools necessary.
- ◇ Ensure that the owner of the scorecard has all the measures, goals, and owners recorded.
- ◇ Trello setup:
    - Get familiarized with Trello using the online documentation and training resources at www.trello.com.
    - Create a new team and copy all the boards from the icube™ templates at https://trello.com/icubetemplates.
    - Ensure that all team members have devices with Internet access that can run Trello.
    - Invite all team members to join Trello, add them to the team, and ensure that they are able to login and see all the boards before the tactical meetings start.
    - Review all the other boards in the templates, especially the Intelligence board, to see sample Functional Framework and Scorecard files.
- ◇ Meeting Plan
    - Set up a day, time, and place for the weekly meeting of all team members.

- Review meeting agenda and process and all to-dos from Chapter 6 before conducting the first tactical meeting.

Our next station on the icube™ train is the tactical meeting beat. This is where the team ensures collaboration and execution of the strategy that is laid out during Intensity Day.

6: Weekly Tactical Meetings

"Folks! Being in the same room but doing your
own thing doesn't make it a meeting."

After the completion of the Intensity Day session, the first order of business is to set up the weekly tactical meeting. As we will see later in the chapter, this is the foundation upon which all of icube™ rests and is the single most important practice that a team should establish to ensure its success.

Light Craft in the Spotlight

Light Craft's team had scheduled their tactical team meetings on Friday afternoons as a close to the week's activities. They called their tactical meeting "Laser" and their strategic meeting "Floodlight." Diana wondered if her team felt the same mix of excitement and trepidation after Intensity Day as she did, not to mention being both energized and exhausted. She was glad that they decided to the session on a Friday. *That was quite a bit of work. I'm surely going to need the weekend to recover from this thing!* Diana sank into the driver's seat of her car, feeling tremendous relief that the team's work had been captured and updated on the Trello boards. Then she noticed something she hadn't felt in a long time: a sense of lightness heading into the weekend. She made a mental note to ask Robert if he had felt the same way after Intensity Day next time they got together. As she drove home, she looked forward to spending time with her family.

The following Monday, she reviewed the Trello boards for the company and marveled at how much they had accomplished. For the first time, they had a Functional Framework that made sense, an audit of all their major tools and processes, and a set of numbers that they could start tracking. She decided that the best way forward was to serve as a shining example for the rest of the team. She would finish her to-dos and then encourage her team to do the same, in that order. Diana opened her calendar and set aside time for the tasks. Feeling comfortable that she was ready for the first *Laser*, she proceeded to tackle the rest of her day.

Build Status Check-in

Vision Track

- ◇ How are you feeling now that you've taken some of the actions suggested in the previous chapter?
- ◇ Did your reflection raise additional questions or bring about more clarity?
- ◇ Are there any issues that you would like to add to your own issues list?

Action Track

- ◇ Have you completed all the to-dos from the previous chapter?
- ◇ Are there any issues that you need to address?
- ◇ What roadblocks did you encounter?
- ◇ If you didn't finish, what needs to happen in order for you to complete them?

The Single Most Important Factor to Ensure Success

In my experience with facilitating icube™ across companies of all shapes and sizes, the most critical predictor for ongoing success is effective meetings. Meetings are where human collaboration takes place. While well-run meetings are not the only factor necessary for maximizing profitable growth, they are most definitely required. Nowhere is this more apparent than in fast-moving, fast-growing companies in highly competitive industries with intricate information flows. Larger companies are more complex; therefore, it is even more critical to have a strong framework of effectiveness across the entire organization.

In the book, *An American Icon*, by Bryce Hoffman, we learn of Alan Mulally's now famous weekly Business Plan Review (BPR) meetings that were established at Ford Motor Company during a particularly tenuous period in its century-plus long tenure. In writer Rik Kirkland's November 2013 interview with Mulally for McKinsey and Company's online publication, he says, "When Alan Mulally was named president and CEO of Ford in 2006, the famous American automaker was on the brink of bankruptcy. The company was preparing to post the biggest annual loss in its 103-year history—$12.7 billion." Mulally attributes the company's turnaround to these BPRs. They were instrumental in transforming the culture by encouraging transparency, open communications, and peer accountability. Business Plan Reviews also set the bar for a whole new approach to meetings across America. And what is true of a Fortune 500 company like Ford is true for your company. If you have *people* in your company, irrespective of the size of your team, you need effective meetings to prosper.

As we learned in the earlier chapter, the Intensity of the organization is determined by a Strategic Planning Beat and a Tactical Meeting Beat. The former is conducted over a longer duration, monthly, quarterly, bi-annually, or yearly. If you're not sure what works best for your company, start with a combination of quarterly and annual reviews. Quarterly reviews are held every ninety days or so. It is dedicated time for the team to set quarterly Wildly Important Goals (WIGs). There is also a special annual meeting to set WIGs for the year. As you might guess, annual WIGs help inform the quarterly WIGs, and the quarterly WIGs guide the weekly activities. This is how the long-term vision is manifested into reality.

Our focus in this chapter is the Tactical Meeting Beat. Tactical meetings are typically done weekly, as this is a good cadence for most companies. You might have also guessed that for there to be effective strategic meetings, it's necessary to have effective tactical meetings. Tactical meetings like the BPR mentioned above ensure teams get the day-to-day focus they need to execute plans. Consistent focus increases trust, which results in high-performance teams and an inspiring culture.

Why Most Meetings Are Terrible

Why do most people hate attending meetings? While the world around us has changed, we humans have remained largely the same. Our modern environment throws volumes of data and all manner of distractions at us. We are moving at ever-faster speeds and expected to accomplish more and more with less and less time, money, and resources. All this leads to us being super sensitive to demands on our time. The moment something becomes even slightly irrelevant, we disengage completely. So, the first thing we need to do as leaders is to ensure that our meetings are highly engaging and valuable. Here are eight reasons[*] why most meetings don't engage us:

1. Unclear goals
2. Unclear agenda
3. Unclear or weak leadership and/or facilitation
4. Unclear what each individual's participation or contribution is
5. Dominance by one or more team member
6. Lack of accountability and follow-through
7. Poor time management
8. Technology distractions

As you can see, the first four items are all about clarity. Most of us want to know what to expect when we are heading into something. Meetings are no

---

[*] Please reference Robert's story in the Appendix for a review of these eight reasons and how resolving them dramatically improved his company's productivity.

different, so it is incumbent upon the organizer to let each participant know the objectives, the agenda, why they need to attend, and who the facilitator will be. Covering these four points lays the groundwork for a successful meeting. The next four items are all about culture, accountability, respect, and engagement.

Meetings are Not a Spectator Sport

Meetings are supposed to be a collaborative process. If any one person or a small group of participants dominates the conversation, leaving the others just watching, you can be sure that the others will tune out. The meeting facilitator has to be vigilant to ensure that this never happens and may have to proactively engage all attendees to encourage balanced participation.

Meetings Must Result in Follow-through

Sometimes meetings are full of spirited discussions, but there is no tangible follow-through. Every meeting should have clear follow-through, with either action steps or clearly understood direction. After all meetings, the collaborative energy of the team starts declining immediately; therefore, it is critical that there be an agreed-upon method and protocol for assigning and verifying accountability to guarantee follow-through. This sets the stage for high quality, ongoing meetings and a continuous improvement cycle.

If this is not done, the interesting ideas and enthusiasm dissipate only to be replaced by the status quo and the daily grind. Unless there is a method, nothing happens, and things don't move forward. The excitement and high-energy participation by team members is replaced by a lack of engagement, interest, and even cynicism. Left untouched, this kind of dynamic has severe consequences for the team in the form of poor morale, lower productivity, and, ultimately, declining profits for the company as a whole. It's best to never let this happen in the first place or fix it as soon as you witness it!

Meetings Should Be a Promise That Your Time Will Be Well Spent

Time management is another thing that meeting facilitators need to watch. Have you ever been in a meeting that was supposed to end at a particular time, and when it was time to conclude, the proceedings were still lumbering on? If you're like me, you might find yourself fidgeting and constantly looking at your watch. If things keep going, discomfort turns to irritation, and then you're really disengaged. Successful meetings start on time and end on time. And when participants recognize that this is a promise that is kept, trust and engagement levels shoot up. If facilitators successfully address the first seven items, they help create an environment that supports high levels of engagement. And whenever trust and engagement are up, productivity and profit are sure to follow!

In icube™, the meeting board substantially reduces the facilitator's burden. Using this tool, the facilitator is able to manage all aspects of the meeting, including time. This keeps the process simple, and everyone else only has to participate without having other roles. It's proven to be very effective.

It's important to note that we are talking here about regularly scheduled tactical meetings. It's quite possible that there are times when the situation calls for a meeting in response to a crisis or an extraordinary matter of high importance. Here the team is coming together to craft a solution or a response and may not know how long it will take to get there. In such a case, all the items except 7 above still apply; time, on the other hand, will be unknown and the general mindset should be, "All hands on deck until we fix this!" It's also important to note that these kinds of events should be few and far between. If you're experiencing a large number of these "emergency" meetings, something else is going on. Add that as an issue for discussion at the next tactical team meeting and discuss it as a group.

The Devil Is in the Distractions

Finally, as we noted above, technology is a big distraction; hence, all meeting attendees need to do their bit to address this. You may have heard that today's average Smartphone has access to more information than a mainframe had a few decades ago! Where is all this information? The Internet, of course. And with connectivity to that massive ocean of information we call the web, there is bound to be interesting, important, funny, sad, thought-provoking, boring, critical, and urgent information attempting to grab your attention every step of the way.

We all know that it's difficult to pay attention to your phone and have a meaningful conversation with someone. Now imagine trying to do that during a meeting with several other people. It's impossible. Just like you probably don't like talking to someone with his or her head buried in his or her phone, you can be sure that others aren't thrilled when they see you doing it. And as we have seen above, irritation doesn't contribute to engagement and trust.

Phones, tablets, and laptops should be set to stun and safely stowed away for the duration of the meeting. In our connected age, it's hard to imagine, but my experience time and again is that participants don't miss their technology tools in high engagement meetings.

The Four Stages of a Successful Meeting

Now that we know what makes meetings terrible, let's examine what makes them great. It turns out that there are four stages to a successful meeting (see Figure 6.1).

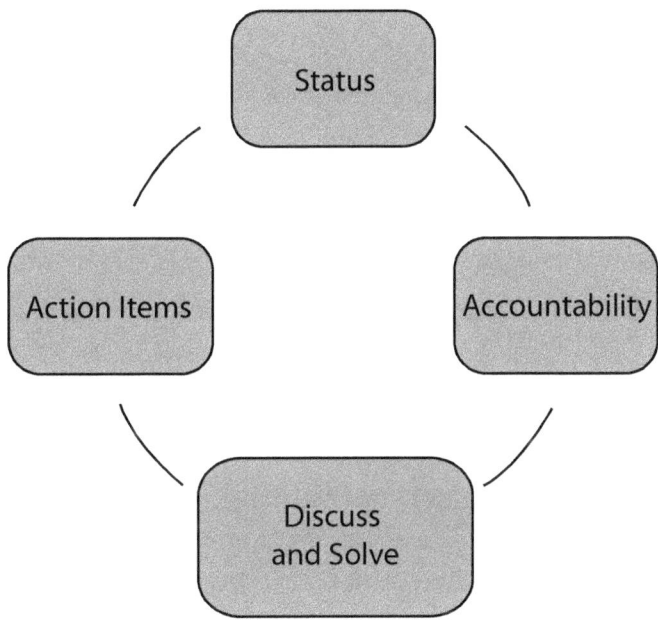

Figure 6.1: The Four Stages of a Successful Meeting

Let's look at these four stages one at a time.

Status

All meetings should open with a clear, shared understanding of the current status. By status we mean situational awareness. Think of this as getting all participants on the same page before the meeting starts. The way we accomplish this is by ensuring that all participants have clarity in regard to meeting goals, agenda, facilitator, and expectations. After that is clear and agreed upon by all, the meeting can move to the next stage.

Accountability

In this stage, participants report on any tasks that they had promised to accomplish prior to the meeting in order to prepare for it. If it's a standing meeting, then it's assumed that these are the to-dos that were assigned at the previous tactical meeting. In either case, this stage is very important to ensure high levels of ownership and engagement.

Discuss and Solve

After the first two stages are completed, the team is now ready to tackle the important business of the meeting. In weekly tactical meetings, this happens in the "Issues" step of the agenda. In this step, the team takes all the important items one by one and solves problems and makes decisions. This process results in specific action items that members of the team have to carry out after the meeting.

Action Items

In this stage, the team reviews all the follow-up work that needs to be done so that members go forth with clarity on each individual task as well as their completion dates. It is best for each to-do to have a single owner even though that person might need help from other members of the team. For standing weekly meetings, each to-do automatically has a due date of the following meeting date unless stated otherwise. This way there are no misunderstandings or opportunities for confusion. Sometimes certain tasks are ongoing or may take longer than the allotted time. In such cases I strongly recommend breaking down the task into smaller steps in order to accomplish something specific by the next meeting date. This develops the habit of getting things done, which is critical for execution. If one item will take longer than the allotted time, this is an indicator that the task must be broken down into smaller steps in order to accomplish it by the next meeting date.

You might have noticed in the figure that the box marked "Discuss and Solve" is much larger than the other boxes. That's intentional. This indicates that all the work and discussion should happen during this stage. The other stages are for support, and the facilitator should be moving the team through them quickly. Team members may want to engage in discussion during the other stages, so it is up to the facilitator to gently remind the team to do so during the "Discuss and Solve" stage. More on that later.

The Tactical Meeting Agenda

Knowing the four stages of a successful *generic* meeting can help us put together the essential elements of a successful *tactical* meeting. If you're not sure how long it needs to be, start with the format below and adjust it to your company's needs after a few iterations of the meeting. You will notice that certain patterns will emerge, and the team will settle into a process that works.

Seven Steps of the Weekly icube™ Tactical Meeting Agenda

Let's look at the seven specific steps that make a tactical meeting highly effective. They are as follows:

1. Opening: 5 minutes
2. Wildly Important Goals (WIG) Review: 5 minutes
3. Numbers: 5 minutes
4. To-do Review: 5 minutes
5. Headlines: 5 minutes
6. Issues: 30/60 minutes*
7. Closing: 5 Minutes

If we compare the stages of the weekly meeting to the stages of a successful meeting described above, the mapping becomes clear:

- ◇ Status includes Opening, WIG Review and Numbers
- ◇ Accountability includes To-Do Review
- ◇ Discuss and Solve is accomplished in Headlines and Issues
- ◇ Action Items are covered in Closing

Now that we have all the stages of an effective meeting captured in our seven-step agenda, let's see how to go about putting it in practice.

---

* Spend sixty minutes on discussion for your ninety-minute (60/90) leadership team meeting and thirty for your sixty-minute (30/60) departmental or sub-team meeting.

How to Facilitate an Effective Tactical Meeting

As we learned in the previous chapter, effective facilitation skills are a critical for successful sessions. The same is true for running effective and useful tactical meetings. Facilitation is an art as well as a science. The science part of facilitation covers having a good set of tools such as the meeting agenda, ground rules, and props used during the meeting. That's the easy stuff. The art is in being able to read the dynamics of the group, play traffic cop (always good), detect cultural issues, and keep the flow. The facilitator doesn't always have to be one of the leaders (Conductor or Promoter), but she or he needs to be influential enough so that she or he is not undermined by either of the leaders. A good facilitator must be able to juggle a few critical tasks simultaneously.

Five Most Important Tasks of a Meeting Facilitator

The following are the five most important tasks of a meeting facilitator:

1. Start and end on time
2. Ensure none of the steps exceeds the allotted time
3. Prevent discussion during the review (Status Stage)
4. Encourage balanced participation from all team members, calling out leaders if necessary to ensure that
5. Maintain a culture of accountability

With this in mind, let's break down the meeting facilitator's actions in each of the seven steps.

Seven Steps of an Effective Tactical Meeting: Facilitator Actions

Earlier we reviewed the seven steps to make tactical meetings effective. Now let's look at the role of the facilitator in following each of these steps so that the meeting stays on track.

1. Opening: 5 minutes
   The objective of the opening is to get all attendees to enter a frame of mind conducive to participating effectively. This includes eliminating

distractions and becoming present. The facilitator opens the meeting by requesting that members put away their cell phones and laptops. Next, he or she asks each participant to share some good personal and professional news.

2. WIG Review: 5 minutes

Next, the facilitator asks each WIG owner for a status check. Each owner responds with either "On track," or "Off track." If a WIG is off track, the facilitator responds with, "Do you wish to move it over*?" If the answer is yes, the facilitator makes a note in the tactical issues list to add the WIG for discussion.

3. Numbers: 5 minutes

Following the WIG Review, the facilitator opens the scorecard to review the weekly numbers. Each numbers owner announces his or her numbers to the rest of the team. The facilitator asks the team if they wish to discuss any of the numbers. If so, the facilitator adds the number to the issues list for discussion.

4. To-do Review: 5 minutes

⋄ After reviewing the numbers, the facilitator goes through the to-do list and brings up each of the to-dos that were assigned at the previous tactical meeting. Participants respond with, "Done" or "Not done." The facilitator asks if the participant wishes to discuss the to-do. If the answer is yes, the to-do is moved to the issues list for discussion.

⋄ If a to-do is not done, and the participant doesn't wish to discuss it, the facilitator should take a moment and ask if it will be

---

* *"Move it over"* is a phrase we use in icube™ to indicate that something needs to be moved to the discussion list and not addressed at that point in time. Typically, the facilitator is vigilant about run-off discussions but "move it over" can be invoked by any member of the team. This is an important social norm because as a member of the team, it's quite possible that a particular item that is currently the subject of a distraction is something related to the facilitator's function in the team. During these times, other team members might need to step in and help move the item over to discussion. This applies not just in the WIG review, but in all steps of the Status phase of a meeting.

completed by the following week. In Trello, the card corresponding to that to-do is marked Red (Pending from Prior).

- ◇ If a to-do is not completed two weeks in a row, then the facilitator should encourage the participant to discuss it and seek the help of the team. At this point, the Conductor of the team may get involved and request to add it to the issues list.

5. Headlines: 5 minutes

   This is the beginning of the Discuss and Solve stage of the meeting. During this step, the facilitator asks all participants if they have any brief headlines they would like to share with the group. With each update, the facilitator asks if the headline should be moved over to the issues list for deeper discussion and potential action and does so if requested.

6. Issues: 30/60 minutes

   Now the team is prepared to discuss and resolve issues using the following process:

   1. Selection

      First the facilitator asks the team to review the issues list and select the top three issues they want to discuss as a group. This could mean that issues that were newly added to the list may move to the top. This is done quickly and shouldn't take more than a few minutes. Ultimately, the Conductor might have to decide the selection and order of the issues.

   2. R-R-R (Review, Roundtable, and Resolve)

      Next the facilitator takes each of the issues and encourages open, honest, and clear discussion on the matter. This is done using the R-R-R process. The first R stands for Review. Here the team members review the issue and agree on the core matter at hand such as the cause and the impact the issue is having on the business. Next, the team engages in a discussion on how the issue might be addressed, potential solutions, etc. Finally, a resolution is decided and the process moves to Assignment. As we discussed earlier, issue resolution is where work gets done and where teamwork is critical. The facilitator must watch for team participation, dynamics, energy and engagement level, and the convergence of a resolution or decision related to the issue.

3. Assignment

    Usually, the resolution of issues results in the need to take one or more action steps. This means that new to-dos are created and added to the list. Here the facilitator ensures that each new to-do has a single owner who has willingly accepted the responsibility to complete that to-do. The to-do is added to Trello with the owner's name and is marked Yellow (New/In Progress).

The team completes the "Selection, R-R-R, and Assignment" cycle as many times as possible during the discussion period. In each of the cycles, the team resolves three issues and creates new to-dos as necessary to ensure complete issue resolution. As the allotted time comes to an end, the facilitator prepares to move to the last step of the meeting.

7. Closing: 5 minutes

    Finally, the team is ready to conclude the meeting, and the facilitator guides the team through following steps:

    1. Review To-dos

        The facilitator shows the meeting participants the to-do list and asks if any clarification is required.

    2. Cascading Messages

        Next the facilitator asks the participants if any communication items have become necessary as a result of the meeting proceedings. These are called cascading messages and may be internal or external. Any such items are added as to-dos with the owner identified as described earlier.

    3. Rating

        Following this, the facilitator asks all participants to rate the meeting from 1–10, 1 being poor and 10 excellent. Meetings are rated using the following criteria:

        ◇ Individual performance

        ◇ Structure/Step/Sequence

        ◇ Process

        ◇ Time

◇ Engagement level

◇ Learning and value

While meeting ratings are subjective and not necessarily 100% scientific, they are a great indicator of the quality of the individual participant's experience. Whenever there is an average rating of 8 or below, this is a good indication of something not quite right that needs exploration.

4. Copy card and archive
In the final step, the facilitator copies the meeting's Conclude card to one with a new date and archives the old card. Now the meeting board is ready for the next tactical meeting, the meeting has adjourned, and participants are able to go about their business.

Implementing the Tactical Meeting in Trello

Creating and maintaining a tactical meeting process is very easy in Trello. This is accomplished by creating a board for the meeting, implementing the steps of the meeting as lists, and creating cards for the individual items such as WIGs, to-dos, and Issues. In addition, we also set up cards for the Opening, Numbers, and Conclude. As an example, refer to Figure 6.2, which is a screenshot of Light Craft Innovation's meeting board after their Intensity Day.

The facilitator displays this meeting board to the rest of the team. If any meeting participants are calling in from a remote site, they can bring up the board on their computers to follow along with the rest of the team. As the meeting progresses, the facilitator moves, adds, or archives cards so that by the time the meeting is concluded, the board is ready for the next meeting. All individual team members have to do is to update their respective cards during the week with status updates or any other information that they would like to share with the rest of the team.

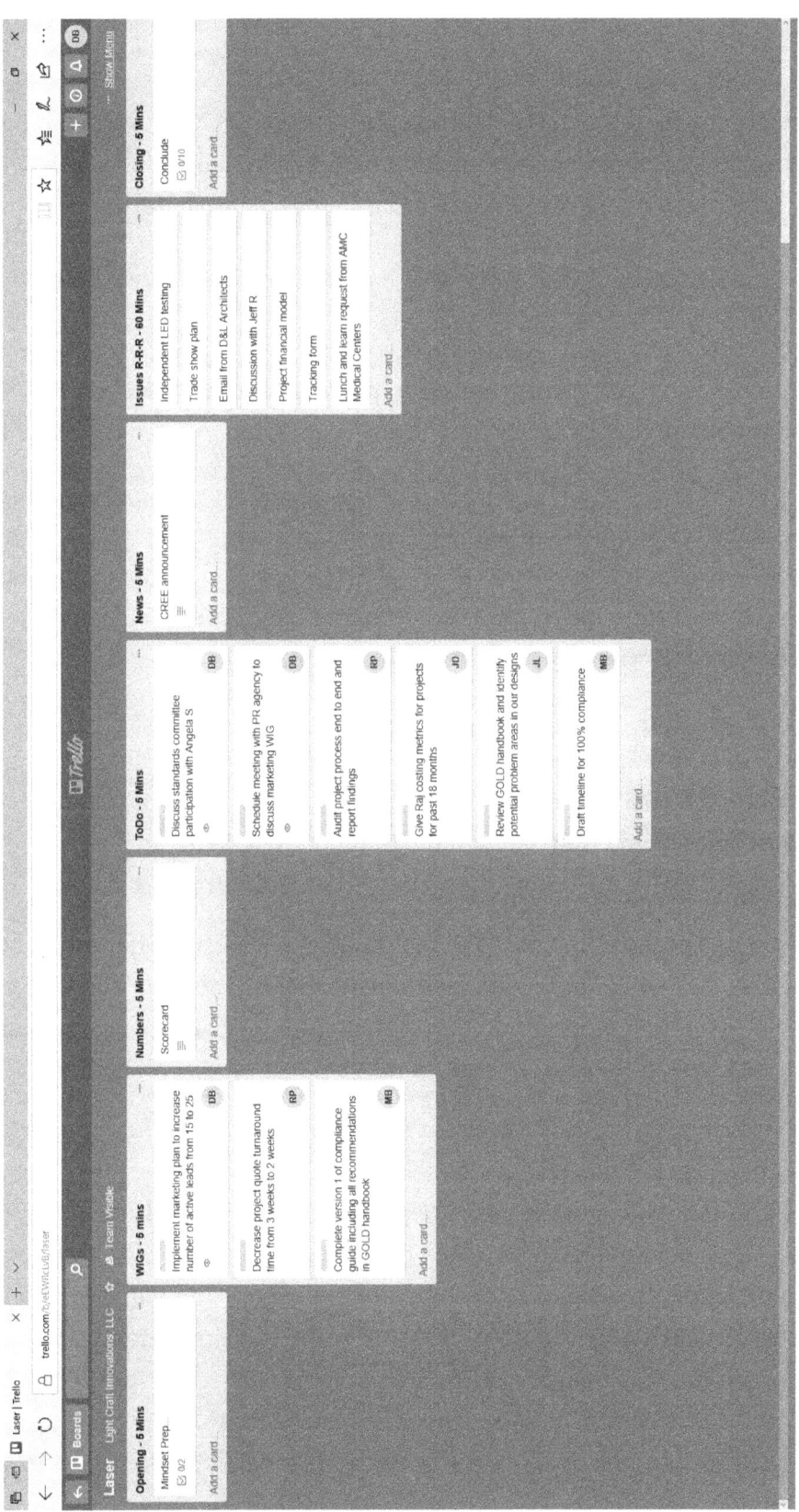

Figure 6.2: Light Craft Innovations' Tactical Trello Meeting Board

Dos of Great Tactical Meetings

While simple, setting up a successful tactical meeting process can often get derailed because of common occurrences in team dynamics and behavior. Hence, it is important to keep the following Dos and Don'ts in mind for the team, especially the facilitator:

1. Create a culture of accountability
   Encourage each team member to participate in creating a culture of accountability. This starts by each person diligently completing the to-dos that are assigned to them in every meeting. Aim to complete all to-dos by the following meeting.

2. Check yourself and your team
   Change begins within one's self. Encourage each team member to take ownership of the culture and follow the meeting process. This makes it a lot easier for facilitation, which is a challenging task.

3. Add to-dos only in the meeting and for attending members.
   Think of to-dos as acceptance of ownership and responsibility as opposed to a top-down assignment of tasks. The only way this can be done is if the owner of the to-do is present and willing to take on the work.

4. Add issues to the list as soon as they arise
   Encourage all team members to add issues to the list as they encounter them in the day-to-day course of doing business. This gets the issue out of sight, but not out of mind. If we don't note something when it occurs, we often lose it, thus losing a potentially important discussion item.

5. Use social norms to enhance engagement and participation
   Social norms are the unwritten rules that we all follow when we are part of a group. It is in some ways the essence of creating a culture. They are a powerful psychological force and can be used effectively for the greater good. Establish solid practices before growing your team. Practices include respect for each other, respect for the meeting, attendance policies, and balanced participation. Every team finds their way into a set of norms differently. In some, there is a consensus-driven process that establishes norms. In others, the leadership helps guide them. In all

cases, the norms are a reflection of the culture, and the leadership team should pay close attention to them.

6. Differentiate between confidence and arrogance
   As we saw in the Intensity Day chapter, confidence is about self-improvement, self-belief, and objectivity, whereas arrogance is perpetuated by comparison, ego, and legends. By legends, I mean unsubstantiated stories that get spread around. For example, maybe a team puts out the word that their product performs better than that of the competition, but no one ever checks to see if this is actually true. Arrogance can then thrive if we do not value objectivity as part of our culture. Confident organizations learn from successes and failure and are good at de-risking.

7. Use metrics to improve the process and not to penalize
   One of the critical success factors for scaling a business is consistency. Consistency can only be achieved by having defined processes. Defined processes are improved by establishing effective metrics. The purpose of metrics is process improvement. They should not be used for personnel management. If the process is solid, the performance by any team member who is the right person in the right seat will also be solid.

Don'ts of Great Tactical Meetings

As equally important as the affirmative actions that we discussed above, we also need to keep in mind practices or dynamics that can be harmful. The following is a list of don'ts that I recommend teams, especially the facilitator, keep in mind. Don't:

1. Ignore to-dos not getting done
   Engage in active and fruitful discussion to understand why to-dos may not be getting done. Evaluate if a particular to-do is inappropriate, and if so, remove it from the list.

2. Add to-dos for members who aren't at the meeting
   Instead, someone else should take it on as a to-do with the task of discussing it with the person who may be best suited to do it without any expectation that it will actually be done.

3. Discuss issues during review
   Keep the meeting flow going by gently asking the participant if he or she would like to move the item over.

4. Allow frequent meeting cancellations
   Set up the weekly meeting at a time when the likelihood of it being cancelled because of other "important" things is minimized. Mondays and Fridays are great for having tactical meetings as they can either kickoff or wrap up the week. Also, companies are generally less likely to have outside events on these days.

5. Personalize failure and success
   Failure and success should both be used as learning opportunities resulting in recalibration as necessary. Taking either of these types of outcomes personally can result in the organization leaning toward the side of arrogance on the arrogance/confidence continuum. This can be very dangerous in the long term.

Coffee Talk with Robert

The weekly meetings at Light Craft were finally going smoothly. After the third "Laser," Diana noticed the team settling into some observable behaviors. The first was that all of them were referring to the meeting by name. The previous afternoon she overheard Raj asking Jackie if she needed a hand with her to-dos for the next "Laser." She smiled to herself and remembered a comment Robert had made when he said to her that his team had similarly embraced their weekly meeting. At the time she didn't get it, but now it made perfect sense. *Pretty cool*, she mused silently.

She was looking forward to catching up with Robert that afternoon. It had been several weeks since they had seen each other, and aside from exchanging some updates about Light Craft's Intensity Day, they had been quite immersed in their own worlds. It would be good to come up for air.

Robert was already at the coffee shop and in line when Diana pulled up into the parking lot. He waited for her to come in. After pleasantries, they settled into a quiet spot, each armed with a caffeine-laced libation.

"Is that a new burst of energy I'm seeing?" Robert opened with a warm smile.

"Aren't you the astute observer?" Diana replied, with an equally radiant smile. "Well, the Global Organization of Lighting Designers (GOLD) has asked Light Craft to chair the committee for commercial LED lighting standards. It's going to have companies from Canada, Germany, Italy, and Japan. It's practically the 'Who's who' of lighting design. Not only are we going to hang with the cool kids, but we're going to lead the fashion parade so to speak!"

"Wow, that's incredible, Diana. I'm so happy for you!" Robert exclaimed.

"Thanks! You'll also be happy to know that part of this is because we decided at our first meeting that Light Craft should make this a to-do—owned by me—and continue the dialogue with GOLD. This might lead to a WIG during the next quarter" Diana continued.

"That's really cool. I'm glad that you're seeing dividends from icube™ already."

"I don't need any more convincing. Our meetings are awesome now. Just yesterday I heard Raj actually referring to it by name. By the way, we call it Laser."

"How apropos! So, are you ready to share any thoughts and insight on the process so far? I remember when we went through our process. I was blown away and had feelings I hadn't experienced in a long time."

"Yes!" Diana exclaimed. "You know, it was interesting. Right after Intensity Day, even though it was . . . intense, I did have this feeling of lightness. Did you feel that?"

"Close. I think it was your mind feeling settled that things were starting to get more organized. I know I felt that A2Z was finally getting its housekeeping done after a long time. We actually stumbled onto icube™ because we faced a situation that I realized I couldn't really handle on my own. I believed that the company was on autopilot and everything was okay. And it was. But this was a crisis* (See Appendix for back story) I had never faced before, and I needed the smarts of the whole team. That's when I had to schedule a team meeting even though I did so kicking and screaming!" Robert continued, "After that meeting and seeing how we put a plan in place, solved the problem, and came together as team, I decided that the company had wandered into new territory. We needed this type of team collaboration to continue to manage all aspects of the business. That's when we decided to put icube™ in place for the company."

"That makes sense," agreed Diana. "If it wasn't for my feeling drained and calling you, I would never have looked into icube™. So tell me, who facilitates your meetings? I mean, I see that you're the classic Promoter. Since I've met all your team members, if I were to guess, Mark's probably your Conductor, but I don't necessarily see him as the greatest facilitator."

"Now who's being astute?" Robert smiled. "I can see you have read my team members well. And you're right. Mark is the conductor. Dave is in charge of procurement, Alice is finance, and Donna is field sales. That's our leadership team, and our tactical meeting is called Power Band. It's automotive geek-speak for the most efficient operating range of an engine. And we see ourselves as a band! But to answer your question, Alice facilitates our meetings. She is the most organized and able to whiz through our Trello board with ease. She also keeps the meeting flowing really well. And you know Alice can be very persistent. She doesn't let up on those to-dos. We pretty much get them done every week."

"Was that how it was right from the beginning?"

"Actually, no. Initially, we thought that as the Conductor it would make sense for Mark to facilitate. And while it wasn't bad, we really weren't firing on all cylinders as a team. That's when we added the meeting quality to the issues list and discussed it. The open discussion led to us saying, 'Let's give someone else a chance,' and Alice volunteered. We haven't looked back since."

"Anything else that stands out that you think Light Craft would benefit from?"

"Keep those to-dos going and don't discuss them during review! I know I have a tendency to jump right into things but having that discipline is critical. Alice keeps us all in check," replied Robert.

They spent the next few minutes bringing each other up to speed on their families and other interesting goings on in the business. Finally, it was time to say goodbye. Diana and Robert set a date in their calendars to meet again after Light Craft's vision building and positioning and branding workshops. With that they walked to their cars looking forward to welcoming the weekend.

Vision Track

- ◇ How are you feeling right now?
- ◇ Are there any tactical and/or strategic issues that you have identified?

Action Track To-Dos

- ◇ Is everything in place to start your meetings?
  - ◇ Review the list from Chapter 5.
- ◇ Is Trello set up?
  - ◇ Make a copy of the board from: https://trello.com/b/j7EpdLH4/template-intensity-leadership-team-tactical-meeting-beat
    Add all team members and have them login and verify access.
  - ◇ Add all WIGs, to-dos, and Issues as well as the Scorecard from Intensity Day.
- ◇ Do you have the day, place, and time reserved?
  - ◇ Ensure that all team members are able to attend.
  - ◇ Clear all calendars.

Effective meetings are by far the most important practice for a team to establish. And now that you know how to have great Intensity in the form of excellent meetings, the team can build on this foundation by tackling Inspiration and Intelligence. That's where we will go next!

SECTION 4: CONSTRUCTION

"You've got to think about big things while you're doing small things, so that all the small things go in the right direction."

—Alvin Toffler

7: Vision Building and Branding

"It's the biggest building on the block. You can't miss it!

Light Craft in the Spotlight

Diana reflected back on the weeks since the Light Craft team began icube™. They had a great Intensity Day followed by several successful *Laser* tactical meetings. Their 90-day WIGs appeared to be on track. For the first time in a few years, Diana found herself having the time to daydream. And when she looked for things to do, she found that they were either being managed by other people or no longer issues. *This is unusual. How come I have all this time? Am I missing something?*

She brushed the thought out of her mind and called Pam Schaffer, their icube™ facilitator, and scheduled Light Craft's vision-building, positioning and branding workshops. After getting some potential dates from Pam, she opened up the *Laser* Trello board and added them to a card in the discussion list. After convincing herself that she didn't have any fires to fight, she settled down in her chair and opened the lighting standards document she had been working on for her own 90-day WIG and got to work. With Diana feeling more settled, now take a moment to reflect on how you are feeling.

Build Status Check-in

Vision Track

- How are you feeling now that you've taken some of the actions suggested in the previous chapter?

- Did your reflection raise additional questions or bring about more clarity?

- Are there any issues that you would like to add to your own issues list?

Action Track

- Have you completed all the to-dos from the previous chapter?

- Are there any issues that you need to address?

- What roadblocks did you encounter?

- If you didn't finish, what needs to happen in order for you to complete them?

With the weekly tactical meetings occurring regularly, the leadership team is now able to use this foundation upon which to base the four elements of *Inspiration*:

- Purpose
- Vision
- Values
- Trust

They are also ready to articulate the external facing elements of *Intelligence*:

- ◇ Customer
- ◇ Value Proposition
- ◇ Product or Service

This is accomplished through two facilitated sessions:

1. Vision Building Workshop
2. Positioning and Branding Workshop

Let's look at these four components more closely.

The Four Components of Inspiration

Just like Intensity Day, the vision-building workshop is a facilitated session in which the team delves into the core of their company, its Inspiration. As described in Chapter 3, the components of Inspiration are as follows:

- ◇ Purpose
- ◇ Vision
- ◇ Values
- ◇ Trust

The team defines the first three so that there is clarity on all levels. The fourth one is the outcome we wish to see. As we have seen earlier, trust is the foundational component necessary to building a learning organization that thrives and prospers.

Vision-Building Workshop

This session usually takes a few hours and can be bundled with the positioning and brand strategy workshop described later in this chapter. The vision-building workshop can be done in the morning and the positioning and brand strategy in the afternoon. This keeps the momentum going and can be easier to schedule for the team.

The preparations in terms of location, facility, and amenities are identical to that of the Intensity Day session. The agenda for the vision-building workshop is as follows:

1. Check-in
2. Situational Review
3. The Seven Mission Questions
4. Crafting the Mission Statement
5. Long-term Vision
6. Mid-term Vision: Three Years Out
7. Short-term Vision: In One Year
8. Closing

In this session, you will notice that there are no guidelines or specific times within which each of the agenda items is covered. As with Intensity Day, the facilitator remains vigilant to ensure that the discussion is moving forward smoothly, always keeping an eye for tangential topics or ideas that should be added to the issues list. Now let's review each agenda item.

1. Check-in

    Check-in establishes the dynamics of the session. Refer to Chapter 5 on the specifics of how to ensure a successful start.

2. Situational Review

    This is a free-form discussion about the company's current situation and environment. The facilitator can start by asking the team questions like the following:

    ◇ What's going on?

    ◇ How would you describe the environment your business is currently facing?

    ◇ What's happening with customers?

    ◇ What's happening with vendors and suppliers?

    ◇ What opportunities and challenges is the business facing?

The objective is to get the team to agree upon a "narrative" of what is going on with the business and to uncover and areas of misunderstanding or differing interpretations of conditions. If the facilitator is able to get agreement, the team settles down with a unified view. If not, the facilitator uses the Issues List to capture important items. This helps bring these conditions into awareness and sets the team up for more meaningful exchanges throughout the rest of the session. The facilitator can capture the main points of the situational review using a flip chart or electronic document projected on a screen so that the team can refer back to them should the need arise.

3. The Seven Mission Questions

   After the Situational Review, the team is now ready to put in place all the elements needed to craft a meaningful mission statement. This is accomplished by using the seven-question approach described below:

   1. Who are we?

      This seemingly simple question is a powerful tool for the team to converge on a unifying identity. The answer to this question can help the team uncover its most essential and primary attributes such as:

      ◇ Skills: experts in electronics

      ◇ Cause: committed to childhood education

      ◇ Belief: 3D printing is the next big thing in manufacturing

      However the team answers the question, it is essential that everyone is on the same page. If not, the facilitator records any open issues and also records a version that is acceptable to everyone before going to the next question.

   2. What is our purpose?

      With agreement on the Who, we now answer the next question about what drives, motivates, and inspires the team. Here, too, the facilitator seeks to capture a unifying theme while keeping an eye on any issues. When it comes to defining purpose, I recommend leadership teams pay attention to the human context in the purpose. Companies that describe their purpose from the perspective of a technology or strategy tend to hold on to irrelevant products or failing business models. For example, Kodak, the leading manufacturer of photographic film was the company that invented the digital camera. However, it didn't commercialize the technology for fear of cannibalizing the core film business. As digital cameras have become the tools of choice for amateurs and professionals alike, the company has shrunk to a fraction of its size. If they had defined their purpose as *helping people save and share memories*, perhaps the outcome would have been different.

3. How do we achieve our purpose?
   This is the first glimpse into the team's approach to accomplishing their aspiration. Here the facilitator guides the team to get the language "just right." If it's too specific, then the team might stray into defining products and services that are best developed in the Intelligence or strategy of the company. If it's too generic, then it risks being too abstract and of limited value to guide the team and the rest of the company.

4. Who do we impact?
   You will notice that the first three questions are internal facing and all about the team, its motivation, and methods. With this question, the facilitator guides the team to look outward and begins by asking the team to identify who they impact. While this question is primarily about customers, sometimes it may be important to mention other groups such as stakeholders, customers's customers, members of the community, etc. Having visibility and clarity into impact helps the team identify the beneficiaries of its efforts and gives meaning to its purpose.

5. Why are our efforts important?
   While the second question is about the *internal* "why," this is about the *external* "why." Answering this question helps the team articulate what it means to those impacted by its efforts.

6. How are we different?
   With this question, the team answers what makes it unique. This could be anything from a collection of skillsets, unique technology,

culture, etc. The idea here is to help the team articulate its collective individuality and make its mark.

7. What are the core values that guide us?
Core values are the three to five guiding principles that every team member embodies. The objective of defining core values is that they define the code by which the team conducts itself. When everyone is clear and follows the code, it solidifies trust, improves execution, and, ultimately maximizes profit. The facilitator must remember to point out that the core values need to be:

- ◇ Simple and easy to understand and follow.

- ◇ Compelling and clearly aligned with the purpose and impact of the company.

- ◇ Something that the team is already implicitly doing versus the values they aspire to.

Core values are used to ensure that the team has all the Right Persons in it as described in Chapter 5.

With respect to the last bullet, sometimes leadership teams will identify a core value that is not currently being followed but should be. This is where the facilitator needs to challenge the team. Can the team reasonably say that they will all embody the desired core value in a reasonable amount of time and serve as examples for the rest of the company to do the same? If the answer is yes, then this can be added to the list on a probationary basis. However, at the next Strategic Review, during the Trust Review process, it will be very clear if this has, indeed, come to pass. If not, then the core value should be removed from the list. Not doing so opens the risk that the rest of the company will view all the core values as meaningless hollow talk.

4. Crafting the Mission Statement
Having answered the seven questions, the team is now in a position to look at what goes into crafting a meaningful mission statement. The icube™ mission statement format is as follows:

The mission of **<organization>** is to **<how we achieve our purpose>** to enable **<who we impact>** so that **<why our efforts are important>**. We achieve this with a team made up of **<who we are>** differentiated by **<how we are different>** and guided by the following core values: **<Core Values>**

Each of the seven questions answered above plugs into the mission statement. It is quite rare that all the answers recorded in the session will fit cleanly in the format above. Often, the first to-do of the session is to craft the mission statement. This is added to the tactical meeting board. At this point, the facilitator may want to offer the team a short break before continuing with the session. As an example, the mission statement of PCS Insight is as follows:

The mission of PCS Insight is to teach leadership teams icube™ to enable stakeholders and organizations to reach their fullest potential. We achieve this with a team made up of entrepreneurial individuals with an abundance mindset differentiated by a commitment to openness and collaboration and guided by the following core values:

⋄ Attentiveness: We pay attention to the world around us, look past ideology, and seek to understand.

⋄ *Referrability:* We show up on time, do what we say, complete what we start, and say "Please" and "Thank you."

⋄ Service: We serve the people and the planet with respect, humility and compassion (without judgment).

⋄ Growth: We foster an environment of personal and professional growth.

5. Long-term Vision
   While the mission statement reflects action, the long-term vision is an end state. In icube™, the long-term vision serves as the North Star; it is clear but often unachievable. The purpose of the long-term vision is to serve as a consistent guide for the team in case there is every any question as to whether or not a decision or initiative is appropriate. This is accomplished by this simple, compelling, and powerful single sentence.

---

* This is a made-up word, courtesy of Dan Sullivan, Strategic Coach (strategiccoach.com)

An excellent example of a vision statement with meaning is that of Oxfam, an international confederation of seventeen organizations across ninety-four countries. Oxfam's vision statement is " . . . . a just world without poverty" as found on the "About Us: Our Purpose and Beliefs" page on Oxfam International's website. Those five simple words provide clarity and direction without any doubt. As you can see, it's also a lofty goal. Another example of a powerful vision statement is the one used by Microsoft in the early days of the personal computer revolution: "A computer on every desk." One could argue that Microsoft succeeded in reaching that goal practically speaking. But they replaced it with a new mission statement: "Our mission is to empower every person and every organization on the planet to achieve more." A point to make here: in icube™, mission is about action while vision is about state. That format is not always followed by other companies, and they may use them interchangeably. In case you're curious, at PCS Insight, our vision is, "Organizations without human friction."

6. Mid-term Outcomes: Three Years Out

   The mid-term vision helps the team define an achievable manifestation of the long-term vision statement. Typically, three years out, it comprises two sets of desired outcomes:

   ◇ Qualitative: What it looks like
   These are three to five outcomes that describe what the team wants to accomplish in three years. For example, perhaps the company is recognized as the market leader in such and such segment, or it has name recognition and is mentioned in leading industry magazines.

   ◇ Numbers: Measurable goals
   In addition to the qualitative outcomes, the team also articulates measurable goals that are objective indicators of accomplishments, such as revenues of $10 million or higher, gross profit of 55% or higher or a net promoter score of 50 or higher.

Both sets of desired outcomes must be tested against the long-term vision statement for consistency. After that is done, the team can move on to the final topic of the vision-building workshop.

7. Short-term Goals: In One Year

   Having defined the long-term vision and mid-term outcomes, the team can now agree upon the short-term (within one year) goals that set it on the path forward. In this part of the workshop, the team articulates the following:

   ◇ Qualitative: What it looks like

   Similar to the qualitative outcomes described in the mid-term outcomes, the team lists the three to five outcomes that it desires within the next twelve months. These can be closely related to the three-year outcomes with more near-term objectives.

   ◇ Annual WIGs

   Finally, the team defines its Annual WIGs (Wildly Important Goals), using the same format and approach as it did during the Intensity Day session in setting up quarterly WIGs. The annual WIGs ensure the team has clarity and focus required over the short term in order to accomplish its long-term vision and mission. At this point, it's important to do a quick check of the quarterly WIGs set during Intensity Day to ensure they are in alignment with the annual WIGs. Most of the time, this is not an issue. In the event that there is a serious misalignment, this is a strategic issue that needs to be added to the strategic issues list. The facilitator wraps up the set of topics related to vision by assigning the second to-do of the session: Update the Inspiration Trello board with mission, vision, and values.

8. Closing

   The closing of the vision building workshop is similar to that of the Intensity Day. After all the to-dos are recorded, issues categorized, and the session rating recorded, the facilitator wraps up the session.

As mentioned earlier, it often makes sense to do the vision-building, positioning and branding workshops on the same day with the former conducted in the morning and the latter in the afternoon. Before we move on, a quick note to point out is that you can go to the website www.pcsinsight.com for additional resources and pointers on how to make the most of the workshops described in this chapter. Now let's review how to conduct a positioning and branding workshop.

Positioning and Brand Strategy Workshop

This session also usually takes a few hours and can be bundled with the vision-building workshop as described earlier in this chapter. This keeps the momentum going and can be easier to schedule for the team. The agenda for the positioning and brand strategy workshop is as follows:

1. Check-in
2. Marketing and Branding
3. The Three Elements of a Strong Brand
4. The Universal Brand Challenge
5. Situational Review
6. Focus
7. Alignment
8. Linkage
9. Closing

In this session, you will notice that there are no guidelines or specific times within which each of the agenda items is covered. As in earlier sessions, the facilitator remains vigilant to ensure that the discussion is moving forward smoothly, always keeping an eye for tangential topics or ideas that should be added to the issues list.

1. Check-in

    As the first step in the session, the Check-in establishes the dynamics of the session. Refer to Chapter 5 on the specifics of how to ensure a successful start. In this workshop, items 2, 3, and 4 of the agenda are concepts that the facilitator lays out for the team in preparation for a successful workshop. The intent here is to establish some common ground for the team members so they can continue their collaboration. When it comes to marketing, there are many theories, and the thought leadership is ever evolving. In icube™, I have attempted to simplify and distil them into clear, actionable, and understandable concepts for business owners so that they can get the maximum benefit from their marketing dollars. I fully expect some readers who have greater than usual expertise in marketing to be able go beyond this material and establish sophisticated programs and campaigns, but I believe they will experience greater effectiveness if they use the numbers, tactical meetings, strategic planning sessions, and issue resolution disciplines offered in icube™. For those who have not given marketing much consideration, the positioning and brand strategy workshop is the first step in creating an effective marketing strategy using internal or external resources.

2. Marketing and Branding

The generally accepted definition of marketing is that it is the collection of activities to help promote and make available products or services for sale to customers. Most people will agree that activities such as advertising fall under the purview of marketing. In icube™ we describe marketing with the simple definition that *marketing is the distribution of value.*

Branding on the other hand is a little more opaque. Many people equate branding with a logo and the look and feel of the marketing materials. In icube™, our interpretation of what makes a brand is deeper. A brand encapsulates many attributes, some tangible, others not so much. The tangible attributes are ones such as the logo, copy, graphics, look and feel, etc. However, it's the intangible ones that make a brand powerful in the mind of a customer.

In icube™ we define a brand as an *expression of value.* In addition to the tangible attributes described above, the intangible attributes from the perspective of a customer include the following:

◇ Promise

◇ Mental perception

◇ Expectation

◇ Discerned differentiation

◇ Emotional dimension

3. The Three Elements of a Strong Brand

The three elements of a strong brand from the book, *Killer Brands: Create and Market a Brand That Will Annihilate the Competition,* by Frank Lane, include the following:

1. Focus
2. Alignment
3. Linkage

Lane describes how a marketing team can create a brand strategy document to capture the essence of a brand so that it can be nurtured and developed to make it strong. In icube™, we use the essential components of the brand strategy approach and map it to the external elements of strategy, customer, need/value, and product/service as described in Chapter 3. We will also see references to these three elements back to the Functional Framework described in Chapter 5.

Focus

Focus is the unique quality central to the brand and the company that distinguishes it from other players. Even in commodity businesses, there can be something unique in the customer's experience that can be drawn out to make the company and its brand stand out.

Alignment

Alignment can be simply described as delivering what is promised. Often companies make or imply promises in their brands and marketing literature that they do not keep. If this happens, customers will notice and immediately devalue the brand in their minds. Great brands take years to build and seconds to destroy. Ensuring alignment is an ongoing practice, and the leadership team must stay vigilant to anything that can tarnish the company's brand.

Linkage

When focus and alignment are clear, linkage is the messaging and visual elements that imprint the qualities of focus and alignment in the mind of the customer.

When all three of these elements are strong and working in harmony, the brand becomes authentic and strong. And a strong brand is the cornerstone of an effective marketing strategy.

4. The Universal Brand Challenge

   In icube™, we review the Universal Brand Challenge to help us understand the perspective of the customer. All marketers, regardless of their size or influence, face this in some shape or form. To understand this, refer to Figure 7.1.

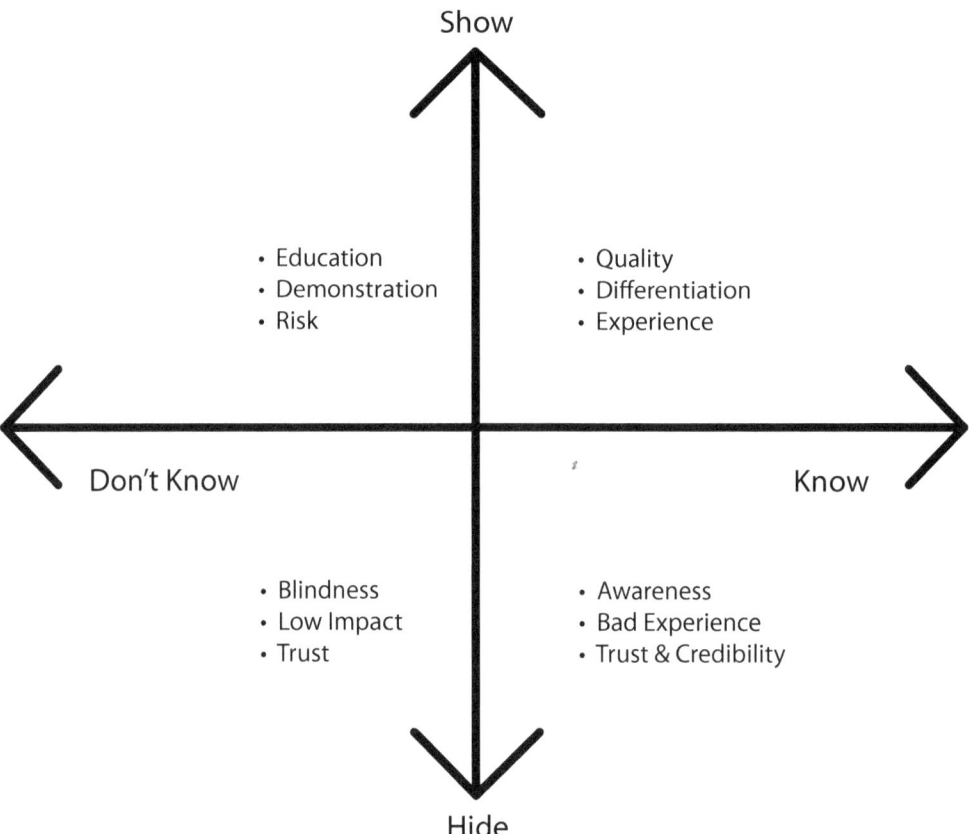

Figure 7.1: The Universal Brand Challenge

In icube™, we identify the three external elements of Intelligence as 1) customer, 2) need and value, 3) product and service. However, when dealing with customers, it is important to determine whether or not they know that they have a need, and also whether or not they are showing their need to you or hiding it. Let's look at what happens in each of the quadrant in the figure.

Know/Hide Quadrant

In the Know/Hide quadrant, a customer may be aware the he or she has need but may not be forthcoming in admitting that need to the marketer. This could be because of a bad experience in addressing the need or perhaps that person just hasn't built enough trust in the marketer to discuss it openly.

Show/Don't Know Quadrant

In the Show/Don't Know quadrant, the customer trusts the marketer but doesn't seem to be acknowledging the need. The marketer sees the need and may need to take time to educate the customer and demonstrate how the solution can benefit the customer. The marketer should also understand the customer's business to be able to discuss any downside risk of implementing the solution and the risk of not implementing the solution. This way the customer can make an informed decision on how to proceed.

Hide/Don't Know Quadrant

The Hide/Don't Know quadrant is potentially very risky for the marketer. There could be many reasons why this is the case. For example, the customer may think the problem isn't important or that it has a low impact, or there may be a lack of trust and misunderstanding on the part of the marketer. Or there may be blindness on the part of the customer. The marketer needs to be very careful in trying to pursue customers in this quadrant as it could be a huge waste of marketing resources.

Show/Know Quadrant

Finally, sales can only occur when the conversation is in the Show/Know quadrant. Here the marketer needs to focus on the quality, differentiation, and experience offered to the customer, all of which are essential elements of the brand and its promise. It's important to note that unless the category of product or service is very mature, substantial numbers of customers might be in quadrants other than Show/Know. Knowing which quadrant the conversation is in provides the marketer with key insight on how to adjust the messaging for successful engagement and lead generation. With this background in place, the facilitator can now proceed with the rest of the workshop.

5. Situational Review

    The Situational Review in this workshop is similar to that of the vision-building workshop. It is free-form discussion during which the facilitator asks the team to articulate the current situation and environment of the company. Here, however, the focus is on determining where the company is relative to the brand challenge described earlier. The facilitator asks the team the following questions:

    ◇ In which quadrant do the conversations occur?

    ◇ What level of trust and credibility does the company have in the eyes of the customer?

    ◇ Are there any other considerations that we need to be aware of?

    As usual, the facilitator uses the Issues List to capture important items and records the situational review in an electronic document that is projected on a screen or uses a flip chart or similar device to capture the main points.

6. Focus

    After the Situational Review is complete, the team is now ready to craft a meaningful positioning statement, which is the essence of Focus, by using the following four-part approach:

    1. Target Audience

        In capturing the target audience, the facilitator encourages the team to identify the key players within the customer base that play the following roles:

        ◇ Decision Makers

        ◇ Economic Buyers

        ◇ End-users

        The people who play these roles are particularly important to know. When they are the same person, the sales process is a lot simpler.

However, depending on the situation, they may be different people. In a large organization for example, the end-user may be an engineer, the decision maker may be the engineering manager, while the economic buyer may be the finance chief. In such a situation, the marketing and sales processes are more challenging, and the marketer needs to be aware of this.

- ◇ Recommenders

- ◇ Influencers

These are roles that are on the periphery of the actual purchase but play an important part in the purchasing process. Recommenders and influencers may be internal parties such as other department heads or external ones such as consultants and industry thought leaders. While not directly participating in the decision-making process, ignoring these players can be risky and may be a blind spot for the marketer.

2. Need
   After the target audience is identified, the facilitator moves the conversation to the area of need. The following questions are asked to uncover the specifics of the value proposition delivered to the customer:

   - ◇ What pain does the customer need to be eliminated? This covers the essence of the value proposition delivered to the customer. By knowing in as great detail as possible the pain that the customer is experiencing, the company is able to articulate the product or service that it needs to deliver to address the pain.

   - ◇ What is the current impact of the customer's pain? Here the facilitator asks the team to put themselves in the shoes of the customer and understand clearly what the impact and overall cost is of the pain. This is a critical piece of information because it provides insight into whether the pain is worth addressing and is a priority or not.

- What key benefit does the customer experience when the pain is eliminated? The key benefit is the upside of addressing the pain. Knowing this in addition to the pain and the impact can help the team articulate a comprehensive value proposition and return on investment profile for the customer in implementing the company's product or service.

3. Product/Service

   In this section, the facilitator encourages the team to articulate the product or service that the company offers in very simple terms. The two questions that we want to answer are:

   - How can we describe our product or service? A simple and easily understood description of the offering of the company.

   - How can we categorize our product or service? A broader classification of products or services in which the company's offerings fits.

4. Differentiated Concept

   The last step in this process is to capture the differentiators of the company's offerings relative to the competition. This is accomplished by answering the following questions:

   - Who is our competition? In describing the competition, it is important that the team has an understanding of the direct competition and also indirect competitive forces. Often for companies that are introducing an innovative or disruptive product, the competition isn't another company, but instead a traditional way of doing things.

   - What is our key differentiator? The key differentiator helps the company define how it is unique in the marketplace. It also helps the customer discern its offerings from other companies and the status quo.

After completing the four-step process, the team is ready to put in place a compelling positioning statement, which is the goal of defining the

Focus. Similar to how we crafted the mission statement, the format of the positioning statement is as follows:

For **<Decision Maker/Economic Buyer/User>** who wants/needs **<Pain to be Eliminated>** our **<Product/Service>** is a **<Category>** that provides **<Key benefit>** unlike **<Competition>**. The **<Product/Service>** is different because of **<Key Differentiator>**.

Since it is rare that all the answers recorded in the session will fit cleanly in the format above, the first to-do of this workshop is to craft the positioning statement. This is added to the tactical meeting board. For your reference, PCS Insight's positioning statement is as follows:

For leaders of growing companies who are hitting the ceiling, PCS Insight has created a facilitated system that provides hands-on tools to reduce human friction while creating value for entrepreneurs, team members, and stakeholders.

Unlike fragmented and piecemeal solutions, icube™ helps break through these obstacles by helping leadership teams align company vision, mission, brand, and execution for sustainable and profitable growth.

At this point, the facilitator may want to offer the team a short break before continuing with the session.

7. Alignment
   Alignment captures the simple concept of "do what we say." Too often the marketing department in a company is isolated from the rest of the organization. When that happens, the clever marketing messages may attract customers to the business, but if the company doesn't deliver on its promises, it can make the messages seem hollow and meaningless. This can destroy the brand. In this section, the facilitator guides the leadership team to articulate the product and service and how it is delivered, starting with the business model:

1. Basic Business Model
   In this, we answer the following questions:

   ◇ Is the product delivered directly to the customer?
   When products or services are delivered to a customer directly, the company has more control over the experience. It also potentially has more responsibility and hence requires more care during delivery.

   ◇ Is it a one time or repeated use type of product?
   Companies that sell products that have a one-time purchase such as a car, essentially have only one opportunity to ensure a great buying experience. On the other hand, when companies sell products or services that can be used repeatedly, such as consumables or cleaning services, every interaction that the customer has with the company can impact its brand value. In some cases, the last order that the company delivers to the customer can define the entire brand image.

2. Product/Service Delivery Strategy
   Here the facilitator ensures that the team is aligned on the experience of the customer relative to the following three questions:

   ◇ How is the product manufactured or the service developed?
   Specifically, we need to have a common understanding, whether it is developed in-house or outsourced, as well as how quality is guaranteed.

   ◇ How is it packaged?

   ◇ How is it delivered?

3. Key Partnerships
   During the delivery of the product or service, are there any partners who can impact the customer experience. If so, list the following:

   ◇ Who is the partner?

   ◇ What is that partner's responsibility? Here we want to know the critical aspects of the partner's responsibilities in the delivery process and how they impact overall quality and customer experience.

- ◇ What is the nature of that partner's interaction with the customer? Related to responsibilities, we want to understand how the customer interactions take place and how they are managed. Since this is a different organization, there may be limited control; hence, it is critical to know what the customer's experience is and how it can be influenced.

- ◇ What are the risks associated with this partner? Finally, based on the responsibilities and interactions, we need to know what risk this poses to the brand and how to mitigate it.

4. Sales Strategy and Process

   In defining the sales strategy, the team needs to ensure that the sales process is true to the brand image that the company wishes to establish. For example, if the company is promising a high-touch, high-information relationship, the sales strategy probably needs to be designed to have sufficient human interaction and tools to capture extensive information about the customer's needs and preferences.

5. Scaling Strategy

   The objective of marketing is to attract a large number of prospects and that of sales is to convert them to paying customers. Assuming then that these objectives are met, the company needs to be able to meet the needs of all customers as it grows. This requires the ability to scale up. Here the team needs to take an honest look at its ability to grow revenues and its product or service delivery capacity without compromising the customer experience. It's one thing to sell one unit, a bit harder to sell ten, and quite a bit more challenging to sell a hundred.

6. Financial Strategy

   Any initiative requires capital. Capital may be internally generated in the form of reinvested earnings, or it can be externally sourced in the form of debt or equity capital. Knowing how much investment and ongoing working capital is needed along with the controls on how the money will be used wisely is critical. The company needs enough capital to be able to make it through a single cycle of marketing (generating leads), sales (converting leads to customers), operations (delivering products or services to customers), and finance (collecting payments from customers) in order to reinvest in the business.

7. Risk Mitigation Strategy

    After considering all the answers in the Alignment discussion, the team identifies all the critical risk factors and mitigation for each of them. As in the other discussions, each of these might be a to-do, a tactical issue, or a strategic issue. All are captured on the appropriate Trello board.

8. Linkage

    The third and final element of the brand strategy is Linkage. This is all about capturing the right message and tone so that the brand has an emotional connection with the customer. Linkage covers the following elements:

    1. Core expectation

        The core expectation is the singular factor that captures the needs and wants of the customer. In icube™'s external facing element of Intelligence, this is the value proposition. Since this is in the mind of the customer, the team must be especially careful to validate their assumption. This can be done most effectively by observing customer behavior.

    2. Brand promise

        With the core expectation in mind, we need to articulate the brand promise by answering the following questions:

        ◇ What does the offering give the customer?

        ◇ What is the brand slogan? A brand slogan is a mini mission statement that captures the essence of the value proposition so that it becomes branded—no pun intended—in the mind of the customer.

M&M candies has a great brand slogan: "Melts in your mouth, not in your hands." Not only does this capture the actual experience of consuming the candy, but it also hints at convenient transportation with a very catchy and easy to remember slogan.

3. Perception

    The perception is the feeling that we want to invoke in the customer as they experience the product. This has three dimensions:

    ◇ The customer sees the offering. This is the perception of the offering itself.

    ◇ The customer is using the offering. This is the perception while experiencing the use of the offering.

    ◇ The customers see themselves using the offering. This is the perception of the external perspective of the customer using the offering. For example, what do you perceive when you see a car, drive a car, and imagine driving a car?

4. Behavioral objective

    Here we answer what we would like the customer to do in order for the business objective to be met. It's important to note that while the ultimate objective might be for the customer to purchase the product or service, the idea here is to capture the intermediate steps to ensure a high-quality experience after a purchase is made. And for that to happen, it might be important to not make a sale if the fit isn't great. Hence, the behavioral objective might be for the customer to actively engage in the sales process that is designed to ensure suitability of the product or service for the customer.

5. Copy strategy

    With the behavioral objective articulated, any copy or written messages should reflect that. Here we answer five questions:

    ◇ What is the encouraged behavior?

    ◇ What is the support for that behavior?

- What is the benefit of the intended behavior?
- What is the emotional dimension?
- What is the advertising tone?

6. Pricing strategy

   The way a product or service is priced sends a message about its quality, effectiveness, and many other dimensions. While it's possible that there may be external forces such as alternatives, competition, and the purchasing capacity of customers that impacts pricing, a clearly thought out pricing strategy is nonetheless important so that every member of the team is on the same page. We do that by answering the following questions:

   - How is the offering priced?
   - What do we want the pricing to convey?
   - What factors, internal or external, impact pricing?

7. Naming strategy

   The first six bullets capture the discrete elements of linkage. The last two, the name and the logo, capture its verbal and visual aggregation. In the naming strategy discussion, we want to articulate anything else that is captured by the name.

8. Logo strategy

   Finally, the logo, often the ultimate representative of the brand, needs to reflect all the essential elements of the branding strategy. Effective logo design is out of the scope of this book. However, having all the pieces of the branding strategy clearly described can give a talented designer the backstory to create a compelling and memorable logo.

9. Closing

   The closing of the positioning and brand strategy workshop is similar to that of the earlier workshops. All the to-dos are recorded, issues categorized, and the session rating recorded, after which the facilitator wraps up the session.

Coffee Talk with Robert

Diana and Robert settled into their usual corner at the coffee shop. It had been a while since they had met, and Robert opened with the observation, "Am I imagining it, or do you have a spring in your step?"

"Not imagining it at all! After we had our Intensity Day, I was pretty pumped up. We have been having our tactical Laser meetings every Friday, and they have been awesome. I can't imagine how we were tracking accountability before. Raj is super thrilled now that all the projects are on track. I didn't think it could get any better, but we just had our vision building and positioning and branding workshop the other day. I thought everyone on our team understood the business the way I did, but I was mistaken! The clarity we now have is amazing," Diana replied.

"That's pretty close to my experience at A2Z. One thing that happened very quickly after we implemented icube™ is that Justin decided he didn't want to be part of the team anymore. Remember Justin?"

"Oh yeah! That was a while back. I didn't realize that he left after you implemented icube™. What was the issue?"

"Well, it became very clear that his heart wasn't in the work. He wasn't doing his to-dos on a regular basis. The interesting thing is that he made the decision himself. I had been worried about his performance for a long time but couldn't bring myself to fire him. He had been with me for a really long time. Ultimately, he came to me and said that he wasn't a good fit for the company. You know what's interesting? We parted on amicable terms, and he is still a friend. He now works as a metalcraft artist, and I bought a couple of pieces of art from him to give as gifts. I don't think that would have been possible if it hadn't been for icube™."

"Wow, that's really cool! You know one thing I have noticed is that I seem to have more time than before. I have actually been able to start working on some neat stuff for GOLD, our lighting designers's association, and it will certainly raise the profile of Light Craft as a forward thinking, cutting-edge company. Is that something you experienced also?"

"Oh yes! For a while there I thought that distribution was an old and mature business model with very little possibility for innovation. Boy, was I wrong! After we implemented icube™, I had all this free time again and went back to my roots of being entrepreneurial and creative. One of the things that I am most thrilled with is our vendor managed inventory system for our key customers. Not only have we been able to further cement our business relationships with these accounts, but we've been able to significantly increase satisfaction and reduce backorders."

"That's incredible. I have a feeling that Light Craft is on a similar path with new opportunities. Can't wait to have our first ninety-day strategic review!"

"Oh, you'll have a blast for sure! That's one thing I really look forward to at A2Z. Why don't we set up a time to catch up again after you have yours?" With that they wrapped up and headed out the door.

Vision Track

- How are you feeling right now?
- Are there any tactical and/or strategic issues that you have identified?

Action Track To-Dos

- Are your meetings effective and occurring regularly?
- Is Trello set up and are team members using it to complete to-dos and collaborate?
- Is the team making progress on all ninety-day WIGs, and are they on track?
- Do you have the day, place, and time reserved for the workshops?
- Ensured that all team members can attend?
- Cleared all calendars?

With successful meetings underway and a clear articulation of the Inspiration and Intelligence of the company, the first iteration of icube™ components is almost complete. We will wrap this up with our first strategic review in the following chapter.

8: Strategic Planning Beat

"Our strategy is to kick it down the road. It's worked for many years."

Light Craft in the Spotlight

Diana's team had been having their tactical meetings regularly for several weeks, had completed their vision-building and positioning branding workshops, and were due for their quarterly review in two weeks. She recalled her last conversation with Robert and how his perception of A2Z was renewed in the light of additional insights following the quarterly review. She wondered if she would have the same experience. She noticed that the team appeared to be getting along much better. And their use of the icube™ boards had substantially reduced the internal email chatter. *The only direct emails I get from my team individually now are of a personal nature, emails from customers or vendors about long-term or strategic planning, or jokes! Most of the fires I was fighting have moved to the meeting board, and I've been able to delegate much more effectively. Sweet!* She glanced at her calendar and felt a thrill of anticipation when she thought about Light Craft's first quarterly review. We'll come back to Light Craft again, but first let's do your check-in.

Build Status Check-in
Vision Track

- How are you feeling now that you've taken some actions suggested in the previous chapter?
- Did your reflection raise additional questions or bring about more clarity?
- Are there any issues that you would like to add to your own issues list?

Action Track

- Are all the to-dos from the previous chapter completed?
- What roadblocks did you encounter?
- Are there any issues that you need to address?
- If you didn't finish, what needs to happen in order for you to complete them?

Goals of the Strategic Meeting Beat

By the end of this chapter, you should be fully equipped to facilitate a strategic review if you feel you have a facilitator with an adequately developed level of skill. If you refer to Figure 3.2, you'll notice that we've covered all the different elements of icube™. To recap, we discussed tactical meetings from Intensity and touched on the internal elements of Intelligence, such as Team, System of Work, and Numbers. Then in our vision-building workshop, we defined the mission statement (purpose), the vision statement, three- and one-year goals (vision), and core values (values), all of which make up the three elements of

Inspiration. In the positioning and branding workshop, we worked on the customer, value proposition, and product and service definitions to help express the brand essence, all of which are external elements of Intelligence. Along the way, we also developed the skills to define issues and categorize them as tactical (short-term) or strategic (long-term). In the Strategic Review, we come full circle to help guide the company's long-term strategic direction. We also ensure whether or not the Inspiration of the company is compelling and powerful and is fostering its final and most critical element, trust.

Just like the tactical meeting beat occurs weekly, the strategic meeting beat occurs quarterly. Every fourth strategic meeting beat is an annual review. The first annual review occurs approximately one year from Intensity Day. You might see a pattern developing here. The weekly to-dos push the company forward into accomplishing the quarterly WIGs (Wildly Important Goals), the quarterly WIGs align with the annual WIGs, and the annual WIGs align with the three-year goal and long-term vision statement.

In a perfect world, we would just set goals once, and everything would fall into place. However, the world is a complex place. We are often subject to forces and events outside our control. Or the assumptions we first make might not be correct. Therefore, such a system needs constant adjustment. This is why we need regular strategic and tactical meeting beats. Every tactical meeting beat provides the team with the day-to-day learning through interaction, collaboration, and accountability, which feeds into the quarterly review, enabling the team to make near-term strategic decisions and subsequent long-term strategic decisions in the annual review. When this discipline and behavior is established, the team will finally be able to realize its goal of becoming the learning organization described in Chapter 3.

Preparing for the Session

Similar to the sessions and workshops covered in Chapters 5 and 7, the strategic review is best accomplished as an off-site, facilitated session. As we covered in the earlier chapters, getting outside the office minimizes disruption and facilitates out-of-the-box thinking because everyone is in a different environment. I would strongly urge you to review the recommendations in Chapter 5 relative to location and facilitation for this session.

Agenda of the Strategic Review

A strategic review session can take anywhere from a few hours to a whole day. Most teams should be able to complete the agenda easily within one business day by using the issues list to stay focused. This helps capture tangential ideas without losing them. The agenda for a strategic review is as follows:

1. Check-in
2. Review WIGs
3. Review Inspiration Board
4. Take Trust Temperature
5. Review Intelligence Resources and Tools
6. Review Tactical Meeting Board
7. Resolve issues
8. Set WIGs for next year (If this is an annual review)
9. Set WIGs for next quarter
10. Review and add any to-dos to Tactical Meeting Board
11. Set up next strategic review
12. Close

As in the earlier session and workshops, these topics don't have set times because times will vary depending on the item, team, and businesses. It is up to the facilitator to use the Issues List effectively to keep the conversation and agenda on track. A good facilitator will also keep an eye on the energy level of the team and use logical break points to give them a chance to stretch and rejuvenate. A rough guideline is to provide a short break every ninety minutes or so and to have refreshments available throughout the session.

Break Down of the Strategic Review Agenda

By the end of this chapter, you should be able to facilitate a strategic review. With that in mind, let's go deeper into each agenda item:

1. Check-in

   The Check-in of the strategic review is similar to the Opening in a tactical meeting. The facilitator opens by asking all participants to take a few minutes to reflect on the period that just concluded, e.g., ninety days for a quarterly review and the past year for an annual review, and report on the following:

   1. Best personal update: This could be an insight, an accomplishment, or just something the participant wishes to highlight to the rest of the group.

   2. Best professional update: This could be a personal project at work, education related to work, or an insight that may be relevant to the team.

   3. What's working and what's not: What's working on the team and what requires improvement.

   4. Pressing Issues: Any other issues that need to be addressed or raised during the issue resolution phase of the session.

   The Check-in is conducted in a round-robin fashion with each participant touching on each of the four items above. The facilitator vigilantly records any issues on the strategic issues list on the Trello board. If an issue is already on the list, there is no need to capture it again, though the facilitator can comment on the issue card.

   Since the facilitator's attention is focused on the conversation and not on the strategic review board, it's possible that duplicates may be recorded. That's okay because they can be can easily be archived or combined with other issues in the Discussion and Issue Resolution portion of the session issues.

2. Review WIGS

   Next, do a quick review of WIGs that were set in the past period, watching for runaway conversations. The facilitator should take each WIG in sequence, state the description, and then directly address the owner and ask him or her if it was done, not done, or if it needs to be moved over to the issues list. This keeps things moving.

If the WIG is done, the owner updates the group on findings and accomplishments as they relate to the WIG. This may be a source of pride, and the facilitator should allow time for this. If it takes more than a few minutes, ask the group if this should be moved over for discussion as it may be leading into the next phase of a completed WIG. At the end of a successful completion report, have the facilitator ask the group if they should discuss the next phase, if any, of a WIG.

If a WIG wasn't completed, the facilitator should ask the owner why it wasn't completed and if it truly was a wildly important goal to begin with. This helps the team understand how to better distinguish WIGs from non-WIGs for future quarters and years. Again, the team decides whether a WIG is moved to the Issues List if it warrants a deeper discussion later in the session.

3. Review Inspiration Board

    The objective of this item on the agenda is to give the team an opportunity to review the elements of Inspiration described earlier. The Trello board should have four distinct lists: Purpose, Vision, Values, and Trust Review. Refer to Figure 8.1 to see a screen shot of a sample Inspiration board.

    Here the facilitator is providing the team members the opportunity to review the mission statement, vision statement and three- and one-year WIGs, and core values with the objective of uncovering any major issues for discussion later in the session. It also sets the tone for the next topic on the agenda, the trust temperature.

4. Take Trust Temperature

    Earlier in this chapter, we reviewed that we cover the first three elements of Inspiration, purpose, vision, and values, in the vision-building workshop. In this part of the session, we focus on trust. As we have seen earlier, trust is a consequence of having common purpose, vision, and values. In the Intensity Day session, the facilitator describes the trust review process, so we won't go into detail again here. During the strategic review, however, we conduct the exercise. Please refer to Chapter 5 for a description of how to conduct a trust review.

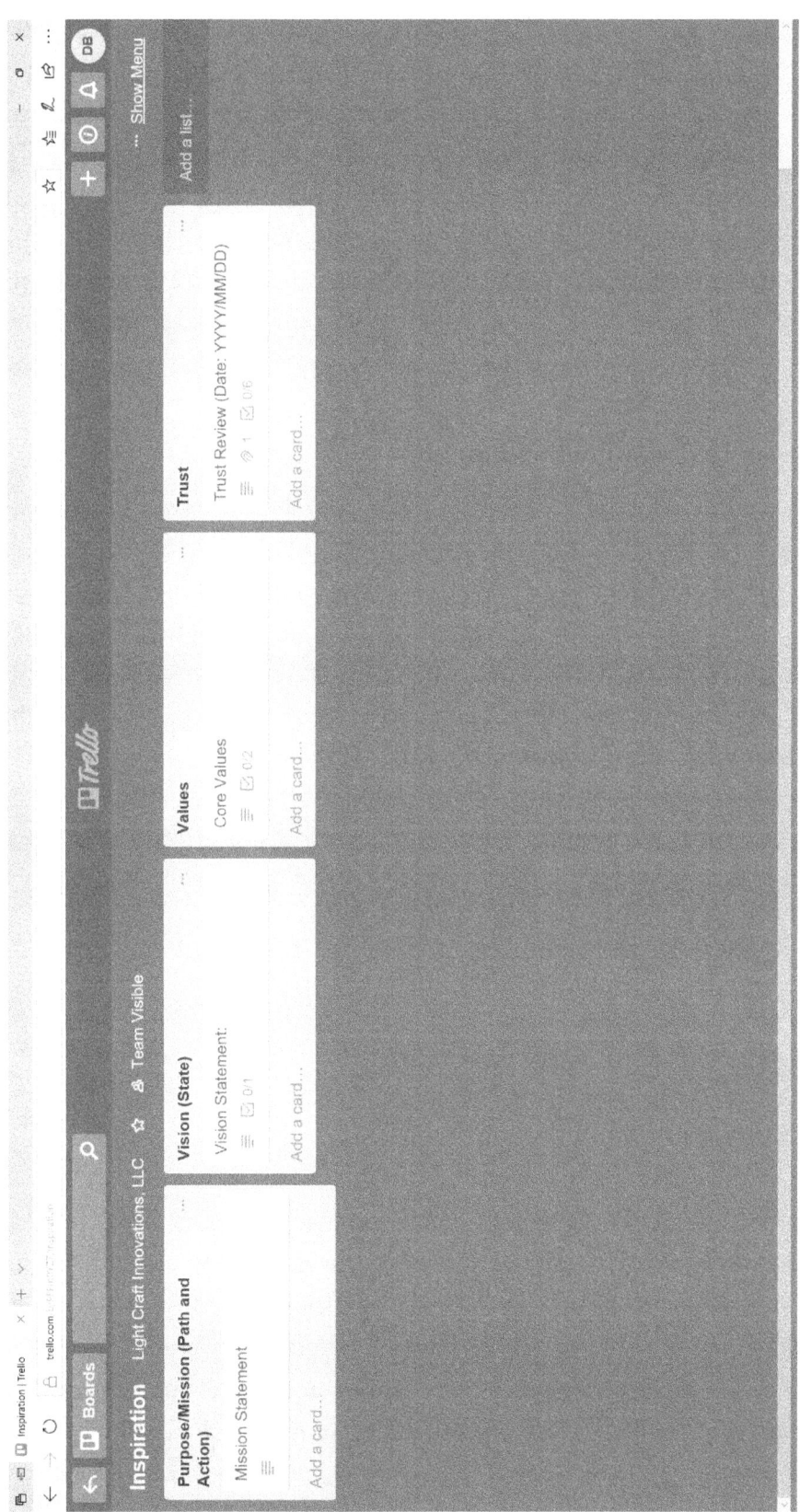

Figure 8.1: Sample Inspiration Board

If important issues relative to any individual's experience or participation on the team are uncovered, the facilitator should move them over to the Issues List to be discussed later. Even so, as this part of the session may take a fair amount of time, it might be suitable to offer the team a break after it is completed. The facilitator should also pay attention to the emotional state of the team as this part of the session can uncover built-up resentments and communication challenges that team members are experiencing. In my experience, teams can have cathartic or breakthrough moments during the Trust Review process.

5. Intelligence Resources and Tools

    After the team is suitably re-energized, the facilitator moves the discussion to reviewing the Intelligence resources and tools. As this deals with the rational elements of the business, many teams find this to be a welcome relief from what may have been deeply personal discussions that took place in the earlier part of the session. During this review, the facilitator provides the team the opportunity to comment on and highlight any issues with the six elements of Intelligence:

    1. Customer
    2. Value proposition
    3. Product/service definition
    4. Team
    5. System of Work
    6. Numbers

It may be useful to ask the team, "Are there any issues or areas of concern relative to our understanding of, or the effectiveness of . . . ?" This provides the team the opportunity to add issues to the Issues List. Even though some of these issues may have been brought up earlier in the session, the facilitator continues to gather issues and make sure that tangential conversations and discussions don't hijack the flow of the session.

6. Review Tactical Meeting Board

    The next step is to review the tactical meeting board and see if there are any issues or items that should be discussed from a strategic standpoint. If the team is running its meetings well, there should be no such items. Occasionally, however, the facilitator might notice that there is a "long-term" to-do on the list, that persistent, stubborn action item that refuses to get completed. Often this is because of other constraints or dependencies, and it may be a good idea to put it on the strategic issues list to discuss. The resolution may be to move it back to the tactical meeting beat board as an issue rather than a to-do.

7. Discussion and Resolve Issues

    By this time, it's possible that most of the morning has elapsed, and it's time for lunch. Depending on the time, the team can break for lunch or use the time before the lunch break to review the Issues List to prioritize the discussion. In doing so, the facilitator is also looking out for issues that are related to each other so that they can be combined into one issue. In some cases, while rare, an issue might actually be two separate but related issues, in which case a splitting might be needed. If the team is using a Trello board to manage issues, then the sorting of issues from most important to least important is quite simple and doing this ahead of time is a great way to get prepared for the actual discussion and resolution process.

    When the team is ready, the facilitator points their attention to the Issues List. They proceed through the R-R-R process described in Chapter 6. Here's a refresher:

    ◇ Review: The issue is put on the table and described so that everyone agrees on the nature of the issue.

    ◇ Roundtable: The team discusses the issue with the facilitator ensuring that the discussion is participatory, stays on track, and is solution focused.

    ◇ Resolve: A solution emerges, and one or more action items are defined. If it is an important and critical issue, it may result in the definition of a quarterly or annual WIG. Or it may be one or more to-dos that are recorded on the tactical meeting board and owned by individual members of the team.

This process continues until the team runs out of issues or steam, whichever comes first, hopefully the former! Of course, facilitators also get tired and need to be aware of their own level of energy to keep pace with the rest of the team. By this time, the direction and priorities of the following quarter (or year of an annual review) should be clear to all team members. Depending on how everyone is feeling, the facilitator may continue with the remainder of the session, which is wrapping up, or offer a break.

8. Set WIGs for the next year (If this is an annual review)
   If the session is an annual review, the facilitator lists the annual WIGs that came out of the session. Sometimes annual WIGs may not have been defined, in which case the team can set those up now. Usually this happens quickly because there is sufficient context from the prior discussion to help define these. As described in the Intensity Day chapter, these should be measurable and few.

9. Set WIGs for the next quarter
   Similarly, the team reviews and defines quarterly WIGs. Then individual team members own each one of them.

10. Review and add any to-dos to Tactical Meeting Board
    Next the team reviews any to-dos that came out of the issue discussion and ensures that they are on the tactical meeting board with the correct owner. Team members who own to-dos can ask for clarification on any item if necessary.

11. Set up next strategic review
    Since everyone on the leadership team is available, it's a great idea for the facilitator to ensure that the next strategic review gets on everybody's calendar. Some teams set these in advance for a whole year, in which case this is just a confirmation. It's also a great time to create a to-do for the right person on the team to follow up on logistics and arrangements for the next review.

12. Close

    Finally, the team is ready to conclude the session and are probably itching to leave. The last exercise is to rate the session from 1 to 10 as described in earlier chapters.

At the end of the first quarterly review, the team will have completed all the elements of icube™ for their organization (Refer to Figure 3.2). From this point on, it is rinse and repeat. The weekly tactical meetings continue as scheduled, and every ninety days or so there is a quarterly review, and once a year an annual review. Now let's see how Light Craft is doing.

Coffee Talk with Robert

Diane was looking forward to her first meeting with Robert after Light Craft's quarterly session. She decided to spend the afternoon away from the office to work on an article for GOLD, so she was already at the coffee shop when Robert arrived with his wife Julie.

"I didn't know you were coming, Julie!" Diana exclaimed with a smile.

"Can't stay, Di', but Robert mentioned that he was meeting you today, and we're going out on a date later, so I thought I'd pop in and say hi before you guys solve all the problems of the world. For what it's worth, Robert can't stop talking about you and all the cool things going on at Light Craft!" said Julie, smiling.

"Well, we have to catch up. I want to learn all the latest that's happening in the world of quantum mechanics so I can sound smart around my team. I'll send you a note."

"You don't need to learn quantum mechanics to sound smart, Diana! It's obvious. But that sounds great. I'll look for your email. Say hi to Eric!" Julie said before leaving.

"Well, hot shot, how are things at Light Craft?" Robert opened.

"Surprisingly calm," Diana replied. "I was just thinking to myself the other day that my email chatter has gone down to a minimum. All the stuff I am responding to is important and generally strategic stuff. All the fires are pretty much gone. Know what I mean?"

"Absolutely! You are experiencing flow!" Robert exclaimed. "In fact, that's exactly what I experienced myself. Of course, I wasn't much of an email guy to begin with. I'm still not. But in my case, it was phone calls. The phone used to ring incessantly, like it was stuck to my ear. Now I spend most of my time on planned calls discussing important stuff for A2Z. I can also spend more time reading industry news, something that I couldn't do before icube™."

"You know, I've been here all afternoon writing my article for GOLD. I would never have been able to do this just a few months back. I feel like I can see through the weeds. The icube™ tools have provided us with a level of team clarity that we just didn't have before. But tell me one thing, Robert. This is just one piece of the experience. What was your biggest aha moment after A2Z started using icube™?"

"It's actually quite interesting. The impact of icube™ has gone so far beyond enabling A2Z to make more money. We have grown consistently year after year and solidified some strong strategic partnerships. We were already doing pretty well before, and, yes, the crisis got me off my butt to do something different, but up until that point things were pretty good. So the biggest aha for me has been that icube™ has made things fun again. In reality, A2Z was slowly burning me out. I often fantasized selling to a larger company and taking Julie on an extended vacation. But Julie loves what she does, so that didn't much appeal to her. She helped me understand that it wasn't the vacation I was seeking, it was the uncertainty and complexity of A2Z that I wanted to give up."

"When that realization hit," he continued, "it helped me act decisively on getting icube™ for A2Z, and we haven't looked back since. Funny thing is that the same people who were frustrating me with their inaction are now bubbling with ideas. And we have a mechanism to channel that enthusiasm into measured and validated action. In fact, I could probably go on a vacation without the company missing a beat and come back energized like the good old days!" Diana nodded.

"Where do we go from here?" she asked.

"Well, it turns out that practicing icube™ is like a martial art. You can always get better. It's a discipline for life. I can see that you are energized and ready to take Light Craft to the next level. The next step is to put in motion the journey that will make you the best promoter that Light Craft can ever have. Two specific things from the icube™ playbook come to mind. One, now that you have all your leaders participating in effective weekly meetings, start implementing departmental team meetings so that the entire company is practicing icube™. Who knows? Light Craft may become big enough that you can add another layer to the organization, and when that happens, you can implement it there as well. The second thing is to be the executive sponsor of the organization to ensure that the tactical and strategic meeting beats stay on track. Pretty soon you will come up on the anniversary of your Intensity Day session and that will be your first annual."

"That sounds really good!" Diana concurred. She felt confident that Light Craft was on a clear path to success, and she also felt excited about the value of her own personal brand with the recognition she was receiving from GOLD. Is your company also on track for a confident, prosperous future?

Vision Track

- How are you feeling right now?
- Are there any tactical and/or strategic issues that you have identified?

Action Track To-Dos

- Is your team prepared for its first quarterly review?
    - Compile a list of everything required to prepare.
- Are the weekly meetings set up and effective?
    - Discuss meeting effectiveness and meeting ratings with the team and see if this leads to new learning.
- Are all the foundational tools created?
    - List out all the tools that have been created and those that have not.
    - Evaluate them for effectiveness and decide if these should be brought up as strategic issues for the quarterly review.

With this chapter, our first iteration of icube™ is complete. In following chapters, we will wrap up with some additional thoughts, next steps, and an introduction to some advanced concepts.

SECTION 5: CLEAN UP

"Success is a journey, not a destination. The doing is often more important than the outcome."

—Arthur Ashe

9: Objections, Costs, and Risks of Using icube™

"We'll have to put that through our decision-making process and get back to you."

Light Craft in the Spotlight

It had been six months since team Light Craft embarked on their icube™ journey. Since then quite a few things had happened. Diana had been appointed to the thought leadership board of GOLD, her industry trade group, and Light Craft had begun a prototype of its own modular lighting fixture system. Mike Burns, head of client delivery, and Raj Patel, leader of research and development, had been talking about this project for years but had never found time to execute it. It would help to differentiate Light Craft from its competitors. Diana was hoping to showcase the system at the next GOLD annual convention. The company had also established tactical team meetings in all the other departments. The leadership team with Jackie as conductor and Diana as promoter met regularly first thing every Monday morning. After a short break, the individual leaders met with their teams in the tactical departmental meetings. Diana met with the business development team, which was responsible for Marketing and Sales. Mike led the project delivery team in managing all active client projects. Raj and the research and development team worked on innovations and special client work commissioned by the project delivery team. Since Diana was responsible for new product conception, she attended the research and development team meetings once a month to ensure that she was in touch with other team members. Similarly, since Mike was responsible for compliance, he and Jackie met during their leadership team meetings as the team saw fit.

During the leadership team meetings, individual team leaders were assigned to-dos for the week. Since this meeting was followed by the departmental team meeting, it was easy for team leaders to share updates with the rest of the team and delegate any aspects of their to-dos to their individual team members. Light Craft innovations only had two layers, so they were able to wrap up all their team meetings by lunchtime. Everyone was on the same page as to the week's imperatives so communication was solid. We will pick up Light Craft's progress again later, but now let's check in on yours.

Build Status Check-in

Vision Track

- ◊ How are you feeling now that you've taken some of the actions suggested in the previous chapter?
- ◊ Did your reflection raise additional questions or bring about more clarity?
- ◊ Are there any issues that you would like to add to your own issues list?

Action Track

- ◇ Have you completed all the to-dos from the previous chapter?
- ◇ Are there any issues that you need to address?
- ◇ What roadblocks did you encounter?
- ◇ If you didn't finish, what needs to happen in order for you to complete them?

The title of this chapter is "Objections, Costs, and Risks of Using icube™." If you're like most business leaders and have made it thus far, you're probably seriously considering whether or not to use icube™ for your company. Some of the factors to consider as you make this decision are broken down as follows:

1. Objections to using icube™
2. Cost and self-facilitation
3. Risks of Facilitating icube™
4. Pros and Cons of Using Trello

Let's take these one at a time.

Objections to Using icube™

As you have probably gleaned by now, I have my own consulting business, PCS Insight, LLC, through which we provide icube™ facilitation services. As in any business, we face objections all the time as to whether or not icube™ would be suitable, useful, valuable, appropriate, (insert your adjective here), for the company or team in question. Since we are not a sales driven company, we strive to uncover whether the objection is authentic or not. If you're the sales leader in your company, you might have an idea what I mean by an authentic objection.

An authentic objection is a genuine doubt perceived by the customer in determining if a particular product or service is a good fit for their needs. The doubt is truly standing in the way of them making the decision to use the offering. An inauthentic objection, however, is when the doubt is just a distraction, and the customer has no intention of actually proceeding with the offering.

Instead, they keep the conversation going so that they can get free consulting from the eager solution provider. At PCS, we have crafted a sales process that effectively eliminates such conversations. As such we do sometimes have to deal with authentic objections.

Before listing out the objections, however, I would like to revisit the Universal Brand Challenge we discussed earlier. Refer to Figure 9.1 that shows the graphic we reviewed in Chapter 7.

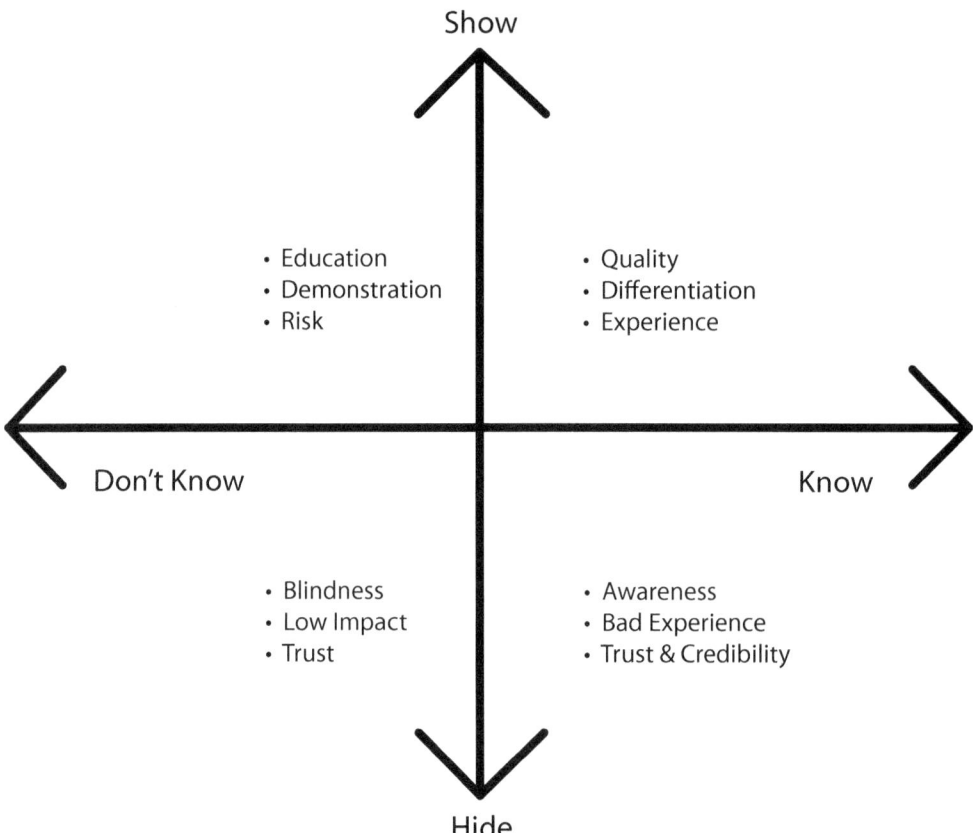

Figure 9.1: The Universal Brand Challenge

The process of countering authentic objections is moving the conversation with the customer from the top-left and bottom-right quadrants into the top-right one. My approach here is very similar. With that let's review the most often seen objections to using icube™

1. This looks too good to be true.

2. We have too much going on.

3. This won't work in my industry.

4. My team isn't smart enough.

Let's take each of them one by one.

1. This looks too good to be true.

The variant of this is, "I don't believe you," in other words, your garden-variety skepticism. Actually, I think this is warranted. Nothing described in this book is rocket science. The concepts and path are simple, though, not easy. The human dynamics make it challenging to implement. And therein lies the power of the icube™ process. It is designed to make a daunting task straight forward so that a team can accomplish the process in bite-sized chunks.

The second point is that I did not invent the concepts. I like to say that this book was written on the shoulders of giants. Many thought leaders over multiple generations have contributed to the principles described in this book. In fact, I have seen writings from the turn of the twentieth century that highlight some of the same ideas, more than a hundred years later. For example, *The Principles of Scientific Management,* by Frederick Winslow Taylor, published in 1911, is an influential text that helped develop many modern management practices. All I have done is to use the best tools available today to help teams accomplish the same goals more easily and more effectively. In summary, icube™ will work if you are motivated to make it work.

2. We have too much going on.

This objection is interesting because it is exactly the situation that icube™ helps prevent if facilitated in advance, but is difficult to overcome if the team is overwhelmed. In this case, the team is a victim of its own success as described in Chapter 3 and Figure 3.1. The best analogy I can think of is of a child stung by a bee but afraid to show it to a doctor because it hurts so much. Eventually, when the doctor does take the stinger out and applies some pain medication, there is relief, but it can appear very daunting before that happens. There is a fear that the "treatment" will hurt as much if not more than the painful problem. Such a situation requires the interpersonal skills of an empathetic clinician to guide her patient to get over the fear.

Let me first start by saying icube™ isn't painful! Second, the journey as described in Chapter 4 and Figure 4.1 is designed to streamline existing activities as quickly as possible. By starting with Intensity or execution, we immediately tackle the issues that are resulting in day-to-day disruption. By minimizing these, we are able to quickly bring some sanity to the organization so that the team can set the stage to address longer-term requirements. In fact, I have had teams come around in as little as two weeks after Intensity Day, the kickoff for the icube™ process, noting that things are markedly different than they used to be.

3. This won't work in my industry

I have to be very careful with this objection as it may have nothing to do with icube™. The principles of icube™ are not related to any specific underlying business model or industry. If the people are working according to their own will and are being led by reasonable, well-intentioned leaders, icube™ will work if facilitated properly.

Sometimes, however, the industry in which a company operates may be threatened. There is little that icube™ can do to turnaround a core business that isn't relevant anymore. Companies grow when there is demand for their services or products. icube™ can't fabricate that. Having said that, icube™ *can* help reposition that company to a different industry or market that is stable or growing by using the skills and capabilities inventory.

A word of caution, though. These transitions take time and resources and are best acted upon when the company has the resources, primarily cash, to stay in the game before such a strategy shift can generate sustainability. We are experiencing a transition similar to this at a sister company, MVS Alliance, as I am writing this. In the previous incarnation of its business model, it was a business software company. Its new business model is using the skills in information management to help leaders select and implement tools to help them run their businesses.

If you have this objection, is it because you have fundamental doubts about the space in which your company operates? If so, before implementing icube™ you will first need to determine how long you have before things become dire. This is a situation similar to what we see in the science fiction movie, *Interstellar,* in which humanity finds itself needing to find an alternative to life on planet earth. As I mentioned before, icube™ might help articulate opportunities, but the critical task is to test them out and implement them *before* running out of time and money.

4. My team isn't smart enough to do this.

Other versions of this replace the word smart with disciplined, sophisticated, capable, competent, interested, driven, etc. This generic objection places the blame on the team when the blame should actually sit squarely on the shoulders of the team leader or leaders. In all my years of working with companies, I have yet to find a team that was fundamentally incapable of understanding and following the principles of icube™. I have, however, on many occasions found teams that were *unwilling*. Why? Distrust.

This distrust of the leadership team and its abilities happens over time, and many things can lead to such a mindset. In family-owned businesses, resentment can breed when family members are treated differently than other employees. In other situations, leaders who are in over their heads might manage by sowing discord within the team with toxic behavior such as spreading rumors and gossip. Or the team may not trust their leaders to successfully help the company navigate out of an industry or relevance challenge. As an outside consultant, I am often privy to "insider" conversations about the leadership at this or that company. In my experience, teams are often mistrustful of the latest "flavor of the week" training, gizmo, process, approach, etc. They have had many trendy things thrown at them in the hopes of fixing "the problem." But if you ask them, they will tell you that the problem is with the leadership. Of course, they would *never* tell the management this because who wants to get fired? But they will say things like *management doesn't really listen*. They will say that the leadership asks for feedback, but then nothing changes. When people see this happen over and over for years on end, they become jaded and mistrustful. This is the most common scenario I have encountered in my years of experience when it comes to distrust of the leadership. Now leaders are asking the teams, yet again, to try one more new "silver bullet," e.g., icube™. Is it any wonder they are mistrustful? Can you blame them? If you think your team isn't smart (or insert your adjective) enough to do this, I must ask, *have you ever considered how your actions and practices might have caused or contributed to you thinking your team is incapable of following icube™?* Only an honest and unvarnished review of all the facts will help you determine how to best address this. A word of advice here from one who has messed up on many occasions: the first time you do this is the hardest. It gets easier over time.

Finally, leaders who don't strive for absolute perfection and don't take themselves too seriously are generally more effective than ones that do. So go for it. It's actually quite liberating!

Cost and Self-Facilitation

The next consideration is often presented as an objection, but I think it deserves its own section for a couple of reasons. First, cost is such a universal consideration yet often not, in my opinion, looked at properly. Second, the cost of icube™ facilitation can vary greatly, depending on how you decide facilitate it. I want to make sure that you have a good understanding of the pros and cons of the options.

The cost of anything can never be considered in isolation. Something is perceived as costly or not depending on the value that the buyer perceives that the product or service provides. Competition with other products or services also influences perception of cost. At the end of the day, icube™, while having the potential to impact the entire organization, is just another offering to be evaluated.

icube™ is hugely beneficial for a company that is already successful but stuck because it hasn't built the structure and systems to tackle the more complex level of team collaboration required for the next growth spurt. In these companies, the utility is high, but they have exhausted their ability to extract any additional value out of their systems and processes. There may not be any other compelling investment opportunities to allocate dollars. To the leaders of these companies, I say confidently, your first step should be to facilitate icube™.

On the other hand, consider a company that hasn't hit the limits of its abilities. Of course, it will benefit from icube™ because all organizations that practice its principles become better, but if the company also has an opportunity to allocate those dollars to something that will tangibly generate more business, then it might make sense to do that first. After all, if the new project succeeds, then the company will be making more money. With the new activities, they will need icube™ even more, making the cost/benefit equation more attractive. So what does it cost? That depends on how you decide to facilitate it.

Three Ways to Facilitate icube™

There are three ways you can facilitate icube™. They are as follows:

1. Hire a professional facilitator
2. Buddy system
3. Self-facilitation

Let's look at the pros and cons of each of these methods.

1. Hiring a professional facilitator

The pros and cons of this approach are as follows:

Pros:

- Service provided exactly as designed and intended by creator of the content
- Seasoned, professional delivery from facilitator with specialized training in facilitation
- Impartial external facilitator to provide fresh insight into company issues and help manage interpersonal dynamics
- Access to latest developments in the methodology and tools
- Access to the PCS Insight, LLC ecosystem of companies

Cons:

- Highest cost

As I mentioned earlier, my company PCS Insight, LLC offers professional icube™ facilitation services. As you might expect, this is the most consistent facilitation experience albeit the most expensive. I understand there is an inherent vested interest for me to position this as the most effective method. That would be true if it weren't for this book. My intent in writing this book is two-fold. For starters, I would like to draw attention to icube™ and attract more business for PCS

Insight. However, I also have a deep desire to share this knowledge with the rest of the business community. icube™ is the result of me assembling ideas, concepts, and principles created and discovered by many before me. This book is a way to open-source this knowledge. The tools made available here are about as comprehensive as they get. Hence, using a professional facilitator is by no means the only way to have an excellent icube™ facilitation experience. By the same token, I have an extensive list of satisfied clients who have found the professional facilitation to be invaluable. See our testimonials pages to hear from a few: http://pcsinsight.com/experiences/. For information on how much it would cost you to have PCS Insight, LLC, provide you with the service, please get in touch with us through our website: http://www.pcsinsight.com.

2. Buddy System

Again, having an external facilitator who is not subject to the unwritten rules of interpersonal dynamics that often occur in teams can be of great benefit. He or she can see things that team members often are unable to see. While hiring a professional facilitator can certainly deliver this, the buddy system method can also do the same.

In this approach that I briefly touched on in Chapter 5, two companies can collaborate so that one member from each company helps facilitate icube™ for the other company. This way companies can swap icube™ services at potentially very little cost and still benefit from the outsider's perspective.

Pros:

◇ Inexpensive and flexible

◇ A potentially impartial, external facilitator to provide fresh insight into company issues and help manage interpersonal dynamics. The reason I say "potentially" is if the facilitator knows members of the team, there's a risk that this person might be a bit less impartial than an external facilitator. You might want to keep that in mind if you do go down this route.

Cons:

◇ Facilitation provided by potentially unskilled facilitator

◇ Interpretation of icube™ practices may be inconsistent

◇ Each "buddy" facilitator has to perform double duty, one as a participant and the other as a facilitator resulting in scheduling challenges

3. Self-facilitation

The last method, self-facilitation, involves designating one of the members of the team with the best facilitation skills to follow the process as described in this book. It's the simplest and easiest way to accomplish this with potentially the biggest benefit being reduced cost.

Pros:

◇ Inexpensive and flexible

Cons

◇ Facilitation provided by potentially unskilled facilitator

◇ Interpretation of icube™ practices may be inconsistent

◇ Potential for counterproductive interpersonal dynamics

◇ Lack of fresh perspective that comes with an external point of view

To wrap this up, I suggest using the buddy system or self-facilitation if your company has other investments opportunities for its capital that could provide it a more tangible and immediate return. On the other hand, if your company is at maximum capacity and is painfully turning away business but generating enough cash, then professional facilitation would make the most sense.

Risks of Facilitating icube™

The third factor to consider is the overall concept of risk. We have seen throughout this book the benefits that facilitating icube™ can bring. Obviously then, the risk of not facilitating icube™ is that the company will not benefit from these improvements. More important, however, it could also lead to the further worsening of conditions that could ultimately harm the business. In the absence of a specific example, I will leave it to you, dear reader, to best evaluate this for your situation. The check-in questions at the beginning and end of every chapter are designed to provide you with insight into these factors.

So what is the risk of facilitating icube™? Can it do any harm? In a word, no. There is nothing in the icube™ process that could be harmful to a company. Having said that, it's entirely possible that icube™ may bring to the surface deep-seated resentments, misconceptions, incorrect beliefs, and other such elements that might be painful to experience. Often when companies are muddling along, these don't appear at the surface, and things keep going as they were. When you facilitate icube™, it can feel like pulling open the curtains and letting sunlight into a room that has not been cleaned in a long time. The suddenly visible dust and disorder can be disconcerting.

Pros and Cons of Using Trello

With the weightiest considerations behind us, the last consideration of whether or not to use Trello is much more administrative in nature. Whenever we facilitate icube™ for a client, we assume we will be using Trello and provide baseline Trello templates that can be customized for your own use. These are available at http://pcsinsight.com/resources/. Perhaps the following Pros and Cons will help in deciding whether or not Trello is a good fit for your team.

Pros:

- ⋄ Inexpensive and flexible

- ⋄ Trello templates designed to support and follow the icube™ methodology

Cons:

- ⋄ New software tool for the team to learn

- ⋄ Company may already have internal tools that could be customized for icube™ such as other software packages that are based on the *Kanban* philosophy

Trello is by no means a requirement. It is entirely up to you whether or not you want to use it, but if you don't have a specific replacement in mind, I recommend starting with Trello. I have found it is valuable and fosters accountability in teams.

Coffee Talk with Robert

Meanwhile at Light Craft, Diana and Robert decided to touch base that week by phone since Robert was traveling home after an event.

"Hey, Robert, how was the event?" asked Diana.

"Really good! Almost made it worth missing our coffee meeting. So I have the next best thing, a latte in my car cupholder!"

"Well, I skipped coffee today, but I have my Earl Grey tea with me. Hey, quick question. When we first went down this path, I know I briefly considered self-facilitation, but it became clear to me that Light Craft could have benefitted from Pam's facilitation. I know that when we talked, you came to the same conclusion with A2Z. So, are there any situations in which it makes sense to self-facilitate?"

"Interesting you should ask, Diana. Remember my buddy Mike Velez from Philament Advisors? He and I started talking about icube™ after we first discussed it. As we talked about his business, their core skills, and situation, it became clear to me that they could self-facilitate. Not that Pam wouldn't have been fabulous for them, as well, but Mike has a consulting company that works on complex client projects. They have the basic skills for successfully facilitating icube™. They just needed the tools and process. Also, they weren't really suffering. Mike is a pretty forward-thinking guy. He saw the problems when they were small and didn't wait until they became big. It didn't take him long to convince his team to use icube™. In fact, they round-robin their meeting facilitation and quarterly reviews. They also do the vision building and positioning and branding workshops at least once annually. It's pretty amazing how he's done it."

"That makes sense, Robert. Clarifies it a lot. All right, sir, why don't you pay attention to the road and listen to something fun? Drive safely!" With that they agreed to make plans to get together soon and hung up. Now let's see how you're doing.

Vision Track

- How are you feeling right now?
- Are you starting to develop a clearer picture on the applicability of icube™ for your business?

Action Track To-Dos

- Do you have any objections to using icube™? List them out and reflect on their degree of impact.
- Consider the state of your company and list out all the factors that make it a candidate for self-facilitation, the buddy system, or professional facilitation.
- If you conclude that self-facilitation is a good fit for your company, can you identify the person on your team who would be the facilitator?
- If you conclude that the buddy system is a good fit for your company, can you think of a company that might be a buddy for your company?
- If you conclude that professional facilitation is a good fit for your company, what questions would you like to ask me or PCS Insight that are still left unanswered? You can email your queries at learnmore@pcsinsight.com.

In the next chapter, we will review some advanced icube™ concepts and the journey beyond.

10: Beyond icube™

"That was awesome! Let's decide which mountain to climb next on the way down!"

Light Craft in the Spotlight

Diana settled into her seat on the flight back from Paris where she had just attended the annual GOLD convention. She was exhausted but pleased that it helped introduce the company as an up-and-coming player on the international stage. Her presentation describing the use of modular components in the design and implementation of high-scale lighting systems was one of the best attended, highly rated events. It cemented Diana as an innovative thought-leader in the industry.

She also formally accepted her nomination to GOLD's prestigious advisory council. In addition to the recognition, she was excited by the business development opportunities. Two companies, one German, and the other based in Singapore, both with impeccable reputations in the industry, had approached her to discuss distribution agreements for Light Craft's lighting components. In addition, she had a stack of business cards each representing a potential design project.

The plane had taxied to the end of the runway, and the captain announced that they were about to takeoff. Diana checked her seatbelt, set her phone to airplane mode, and glanced at her calendar before turning off the screen. Light Craft's annual review was a few weeks away. *It's going to be a busy year,* she thought as she smiled and dozed off. We will catch up with Diana and Robert later in this chapter. Now let's see how you're doing.

Build Status Check-in

Vision Track

- ◇ How are you feeling now that you've taken some of the actions suggested in the previous chapter?
- ◇ Did your reflection raise additional questions or bring about more clarity?
- ◇ Are there any issues that you would like to add to your own issues list?

Action Track

- ◇ Have you completed all the to-dos from the previous chapter?
- ◇ Are there any issues that you need to address?
- ◇ What roadblocks did you encounter?
- ◇ If you didn't finish, what needs to happen in order for you to complete them?

As I have mentioned in earlier chapters, icube™ is a journey, not a destination. Let's review what icube™ is and what it is not, starting with what it is not.

It is not consulting, which usually involves some kind of subject matter expertise related to an industry or business model. icube™ applies to any company in which the core issues described in earlier chapters are manifest.

Along the same lines, icube™ isn't a solution to any given problem or set of problems. Instead, icube™ is a method for organizing human energy so it is conducive to cooperation and collaboration in order to execute and serve a common mission and purpose. From there we can conclude that icube™ isn't really about business at all. It's about people. The principles of icube™ will help any group of people realize a common vision and accomplish their goals. It is an ongoing practice that enables all team members to be on the same page and work effectively as a cohesive unit.

As I wrap up this book, I trust I have provided you with the guidance necessary to decide if icube™ is a good fit for your team, and if so, what you need to successfully transform your business into a prosperous, growing, thriving organization that is a joy to work for. With that in mind, I'd like to leave you with some final follow-up topics to develop in your company:

1. Departmental tactical and strategic meetings beyond the leadership team
2. Advanced scorecard concepts and gainsharing
3. Establishment of a functioning board
4. Effective use of information systems
5. Company growth dynamics

Let's take these one at a time.

Departmental Tactical and Strategic Meetings Beyond the Leadership Team

Though we've already covered the importance of leadership and departmental tactical and strategic meetings, let's look more closely at how the grouping, agenda, and format of these meetings will help the company execute as a whole to maximize its throughput and profits. First let's consider grouping. Refer to Figure 10.1.

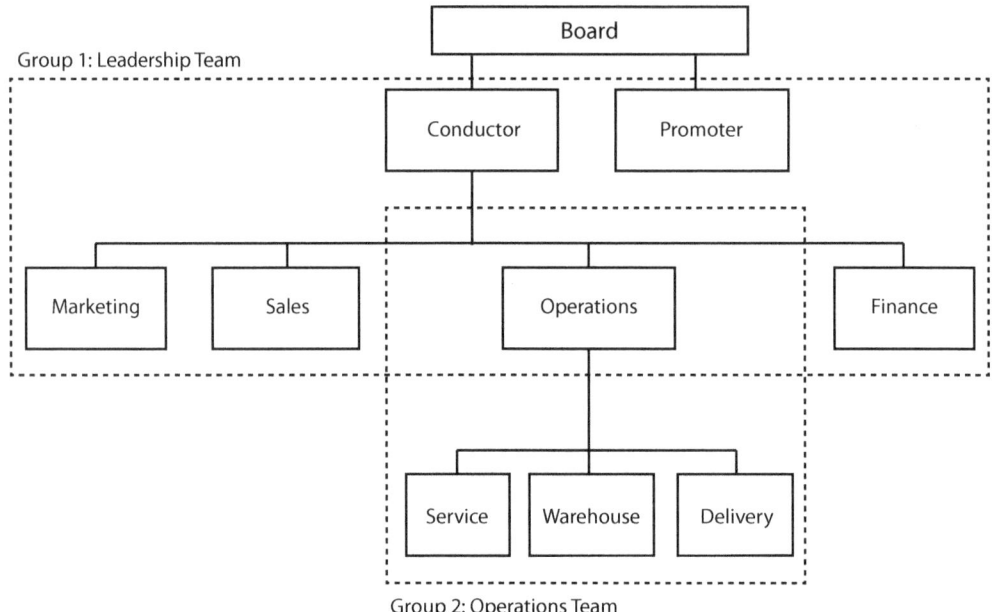

Figure 10.1: Tactical Meeting Groupings

This is the standard icube™ Functional Framework as described in Chapter 5. You will also notice that below the Operations function, we have three additional sub-functions: service, warehouse, and delivery. In this example, Operations is responsible for these three functions to be able to service this company's customers. You will also see two groupings of functions marked by dashed lines.

The first group comprises the functions promoter, conductor, marketing, sales, operations, and finance. You will recognize these as the leadership team. The second group contains operations, service, warehouse, and delivery. As you might have guessed, the first grouping holds leadership team tactical meetings while the second grouping holds operations departmental meetings. Note that operations is in both groupings. Similarly, we can create subgroupings for sales, marketing and finance such as we did for operations.

We accomplish two objectives by creating groupings in this manner. First, this ensures that no one need attend more than two tactical meetings in any given week, thereby sharply reducing the number of meetings growing companies often have when they are not effectively organized. Second, if we schedule the leadership team meeting before departmental meetings, we can easily ensure that any decisions made at the leadership team level are communicated to the departmental teams. Specific items can also be moved from the leadership team's tactical meeting board to any department's tactical issues list for that team to discuss if necessary. This approach radically improves the communication and collaboration for the entire company. This grouping applies to tactical and strategic meetings.

The next item to consider is the agenda and format of the meeting. Let's start with the leadership tactical meeting described in Chapter 6:

1. Opening: 5 minutes
2. Wildly Important Goals (WIG) Review: 5 minutes
3. Numbers: 5 minutes
4. To-dos Review: 5 minutes
5. Headlines: 5 minutes
6. Issues: 60 minutes
7. Closing: 5 Minutes

This agenda allows ninety minutes for the entire meeting. To implement this agenda for a departmental tactical meeting, I recommend three specific actions:

- ◇ Define your team's WIGs
- ◇ Define your team's scorecard
- ◇ Determine appropriate discussion time for issues

Let's review each of these actions.

Define Your Team's WIGs

As we saw in Chapters 5 and 8, after Intensity Day and each quarterly review, the leadership team sets wildly important goals (WIGs). As you would expect, these WIGs are high level and need to be translated into specific WIGs for each of the teams. For example, the company's WIG as a whole might be something like increase sales of widget from X to Y. This WIG could then translate into marketing, sales, operations, and finance WIGS as follows:

- Marketing: Increase exposure of widget in customer base from A to B
- Sales: Develop incentive plan for widget purchases in product line C and D
- Operations: Increase capacity of widget production to Y + 10%
- Finance: Secure working capital for additional widget production

These are just illustrations. Some departments may have additional WIGs to support the company goals.

Define Your Team's Scorecard

We also saw in Chapter 5 how to define a scorecard that becomes an objective measure of the company's performance. At the leadership team level, the scorecard should be detailed enough to grasp how the company is functioning but not be filled with measures that could bog down understanding. Hence, each departmental team should create its own numbers to be effective in internal execution but also provide a *roll-up,* or subset, for the leadership team. For example, let's look at the numbers in the scorecard for the Marketing function:

Marketing Team Numbers:
- Ads commissioned in print (activity)
- Ads commissioned online (activity)
- Emails sent (activity)
- Social media posts (activity)
- Online views (output)
- Email opens (output)
- Media mentions (output)
- Qualified leads (output)

Leadership Team Numbers:
- Advertising spend (input)
- Exposures (output), sum of the online views
- Email opens

◇ Media mentions

◇ Qualified leads (output)

This way the leadership team has all the information it needs to ensure that the business is functioning smoothly at a high level. In the event any team is facing issues, the numbers will show it. At this time, it becomes an issue for the team and most likely something that individual leader needs to follow-up on, potentially off line, with the conductor after referring to the departmental scorecard.

Determine Appropriate Discussion Time for Issues

The team also needs to decide how much time to allocate for Step 6 in the meeting agenda. In Chapter 6, I made a note that leadership team meetings need sixty minutes and departmental meetings could do with thirty minutes. These are just suggestions. If you are not sure, then start with this approach and adjust up as necessary. The idea here is to ensure that all critical and most other real issues are resolved in a timely manner. You will get a sense of the optimal duration after running meetings a few times.

This brings us to departmental strategic meetings. As you might observe, the elements of the tactical meetings considered above are defined during Intensity Day and subsequent strategic reviews. Hence, this same format should be followed in departments, as well.

I recommend that all departments have their own Intensity Day session and quarterly reviews after the leadership team has conducted theirs. If the company has the resources, it should use a professional facilitator. Departmental sessions usually don't take as long as leadership team sessions because the direction of the company has been set. Also, the vision, mission, and brand positioning defined by the leadership team should guide the activities of each department, and unless it's a distinct business unit, vision, mission, and brand positioning statements are usually not required to be redone.

Before we move on to the next section, I want to point out another meeting grouping that you should consider that is not shown in the figure. This is the concept of regular, potentially weekly Promoter/Conductor tactical meetings. At Automation Alley, Tom Kelly (Promoter) and I (Conductor) meet every Friday afternoon to go over the entire business and discuss all the important issues for our leadership team tactical meeting (Directors's Meeting), which is every

Monday morning. We start the meeting with a check-in and conclude with a rating just like any other tactical meeting. As the Promoter and Conductor, this practice keeps us completely aligned. Even though adding one more meeting may appear counter-intuitive, alignment between the two top leaders goes a long way in maximizing the flow and profitability of the company.

Advanced Scorecard Concepts and Gainsharing

When I mention advanced scorecard concepts, I want to point to the thinking behind this, not necessarily the technology. As we discussed in Chapter 5, there are four types of numbers we can measure for any system or component of a system: inputs, outputs, activities, and influencers. Of these, however, the only type of number we can truly control is activities, though we can influence outputs and inputs to a large extent. Finally, having an understanding of the influencers can help us determine how to adjust or adapt our behavior to impact the best outcome.

For example, maybe you are a farmer growing a certain type of crop. You may know the relationship between temperature and water for the plant that you are growing, for example, more water for higher temperatures, less for lower. This makes your job of keeping the plants happy and watered straightforward. You will need a system to measure the temperature (influencer) to determine how much water to put through the irrigation system (activity). The trick is in making measurements over time and understanding the optimum relationship.

Companies are similar systems, and one of the most powerful variables that can make companies highly successful is human engagement. In the Introduction, I discussed how icube™ can help improve team engagement and foster an ownership mindset. Other tools that we have discussed such as the Functional Framework, tactical and strategic meetings, vision-building and positioning and branding sessions, trust reviews, etc., are all intended to help leaders accomplish this goal. Similarly, the scorecard can be a very powerful tool to enable a company to make great strides down this path.

Gainsharing is a practice that companies can follow to ensure high levels of team engagement in conjunction with a well-designed scorecard. Here is a simple definition: Gainsharing is a group incentive system designed to elevate individual fulfillment, team engagement, and productivity, using simple, compelling metrics that are easy to track. A comprehensive description and implementation plan for gainsharing is beyond the scope of this book, but I encourage you to do your own research on this topic. There are many excellent resources on the Internet that will give you a working understanding of the topic.

First introduced by Joseph Scanlon, an MIT lecturer in the first half of the twentieth century, gainsharing has evolved into a practical and powerful method to authentically motivate humans. An effective gainsharing plan has four important elements:

1. Financial reward: other programs may provide different kinds of recognition or rewards.

2. Understandable, easy-to-measure numbers: these are usually non-financial in nature, such as increased production quantities or reduced defects.

3. Group vs. individual focus: an incentive plan is not designed to maximize individual performance as this can lead to unhealthy internal competition.

4. Match reward with performance in the same time frame: gainsharing bonuses are usually paid out bi-weekly or at least monthly.

Well-designed gainsharing systems can effectively *walk the talk* of fostering an ownership mindset by directly connecting team engagement with financial reward.

Establishment of a Functioning Board

Most growing businesses, particularly ones that are closely held and not funded by professional investors like angel groups or venture capital firms, don't have established boards. Of those that do, many aren't set up to make use of the expertise and guidance that a well-functioning board can provide. Often the directors are selected based on personal relationships without a lot of forethought as to the strategic make-up and mix of skill sets, abilities, and connections. On the other hand, when the board of directors functions well as a team, it can do wonders for the long-term growth, strategic direction, and sustainability of an organization. The board serves as the foundational bedrock for an organization's corporate governance practices.

As you might see, the clarity and tools that icube™ provides the leadership team and the rest of the organization below it, can also be expressed and implemented upward toward the board. This can enable the board as well to function as a team in guiding and assisting the leadership team to execute the company's mission. Furthermore, when the leadership team is clear on the firm's mission, vision, and strategic positioning, this can help them identify ideal types of board members with a wide range of competencies, experiences, and industry connections. icube™ often enables leadership teams for the first time to be much more strategic in their selection of directors for the board.

Effective Use of Information Systems

With icube™, the leadership team gets the clarity needed to design a System of Work to maximize throughput. They also get a better understanding of what information systems need to support the processes that make up the System of Work. These decisions can then be tested and validated on an ongoing basis so that the company learns (see Chapter 3) and continuously improves its performance over time.

In Chapter 5, we discussed the importance of creating an effective System of Work. This is the *how* of the internal elements of strategy. An effective System of Work is comprised of processes and tools. Processes are the step-by-step tasks that need to be performed in executing any initiative. Tools are the equipment required to execute a process. A System of Work needs to be designed to account for the Functional Framework (people) and the scorecard (numbers) ensuring that the *how*, *who*, and *how much* are all aligned, thus, ensuring the smooth flow of work throughout the system.

In terms of tools, it is almost impossible to find a process in a modern business that does not manage or execute without the use of computers. Marketing requires a functional website complemented by other tools such as email, newsletters, social media, etc. Sales relies on an effective customer relationship management (CRM) system that may provide functions such as lead management. Sales may also interface with Operations by creating quotes and orders in an order processing system that is part of an enterprise resource and planning (ERP) system. Finally, finance may use components of the ERP system or have a stand-alone finance system to track capital and financial performance. When a company uses icube™, the clarity it achieves relative to the System of Work, Numbers, and Functions within the organization can enable it to effectively select, implement, and configure information systems to maximize throughput and profit.

Company Growth Dynamics

As much as business leaders would like, the growth of companies is rarely a steady process. The graphic in Figure 10.2 tries to explain this.

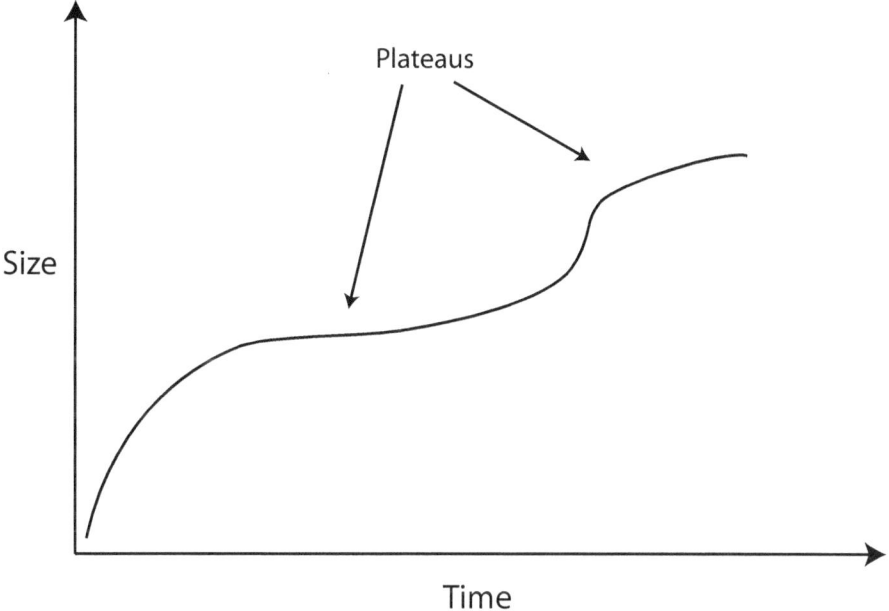

Figure 10.2: How Companies Grow

The horizontal axis is time, and the vertical axis is some indicator of growth such as size. It's important to state here that this is a simplification. There isn't one single measure of size. One measure might be overall sales; however, a company with greater sales than another company may not be as profitable. Another measure might be number of employees. However, that too isn't a good representation since a company that is highly automated may have a smaller number of employees that are highly skilled. The earlier measure of profit alone also isn't a good indicator of the trajectory of a company. For example, Amazon, the Internet retail giant, has consistently reported very low profits and in some cases losses because of the massive amounts of reinvestment, not all of which can be capitalized. In fact, growth and growth prospects are an assessment involving qualitative and quantitative analysis that is the basis of investment analysis.

This is why we will just use the word size. I hope you will have a good sense of what that might mean for your specific organization.

More important, however, is the path of growth that the figure shows. Growth, it turns out, is made up of periods of steady growth followed by periods of what appear to be stagnation or plateaus. During the plateaus, the company hits an invisible ceiling. Only when it is able to break through the ceiling is it able to experience the subsequent stages of growth. This can happen many times over the life of the company. It is also possible that at any of these plateaus might be the end of the rope for the company. In that case, it could either start shrinking or get bought out by another company. The determining factor as to whether or not a company is able to break through is the ability of the leadership team to retool the company during a plateau for the next stage of growth. If facilitated and practiced properly, icube™ can be the catalyst to make this retooling possible at every plateau.

Whenever this happens the leadership team needs to revisit all elements of the company's *Intelligence*, more specifically the internal elements of Team, System of Work, and Numbers, and implement the upgrades necessary to support the growth. A great analogy of this is in the movie *Inside Out*, an innovative animated movie showing the inner workings of the mind of a child. Our protagonist, Riley, is a preteen who has moved from the Midwest to the west coast. Her behavior is influenced by the interactions of five emotions portrayed as characters: joy, anger, disgust, fear, and sadness. Each of these characters manipulates buttons and levers on a control panel. Toward the end of the movie, as our heroine is growing up, her control panel is replaced by a much larger one with many more buttons and levers, representing Riley's growth and maturity. A company's growth is very much like this. It's important to recognize that a small company isn't a miniaturized version of a large company. A large company is significantly more complex. A leadership team can use icube™ to design and implement the structures and systems that are most appropriate for the stage of the company's growth.

Critical icube™ Concepts in a Nutshell

Before closing this book, let's summarize the most important concepts that icube™ teaches:

- ◇ Inspiration, Intelligence, and Intensity in any team are interconnected:
    - Inspiration motivates Intelligence.
    - Intelligence powers Intensity.
    - Intensity sustains Inspiration.
- ◇ Trust is the binding glue of any learning organization that constantly evaluates its Intelligence by continuously validating its offering, Team structure, System of Work, and Numbers.
- ◇ The foundation of Intensity is the quality of meetings that occur within the organization. Tactical meetings are execution oriented and strategic meetings are planning oriented. Meetings can only be useful if they include the following:
    - High level of accountability
    - Trust fostered by Inspiration
    - Effective Functional Framework
    - Great systems
    - Right numbers provided by Intelligence

With this in mind, now let's check in one last time on Diana and Light Craft Innovations.

Coffee Talk with Robert

Diana was finally back in the saddle having recovered from the jetlag she experienced after her trip to Paris. Her next coffee meeting with Robert was a couple of weeks before Light Craft's annual meeting. *I'm not sure exactly what else to discuss at our annual meeting besides the issues I've already added to the review board. Unless I am missing something, everything seems to be under control.*

As they settled down at their favorite table, Robert opened the conversation. "So how are you Diana? How was Paris?"

"Just incredible, Robert!" she beamed and proceeded to update him with everything that had occurred at and since the GOLD convention, including the issues she added to Light Craft's strategic review board for the upcoming annual review.

"That's wonderful to hear, Diana!" he replied. "Light Craft has made an incredible amount of progress over the last year. It's absolutely a delight to watch that happen. I take it the team is doing well?"

"They're firing on all cylinders!"

"Excellent! So anything you wanted to talk about related to Light Craft's upcoming annual review that I can help you with?"

"Honestly, Robert, I can't think of anything. With icube™ humming, we've been able to have a spot for everything. I don't think there's anything specific for us to discuss today."

"Oh, my! Am I not needed anymore?" he joked. "Just kidding. Actually, that doesn't surprise me one bit. I think all the issues you were dealing with were the result of not having the tools in place to deal with Light Craft's growth. Now that you have them, it probably appears more manageable."

"Yes, and so much more enjoyable!" Diana exclaimed. "In fact, Robert, as I was heading back from Paris, I was thinking to myself that I really wasn't doing anything wrong before we started with icube™. The business problems I was facing are not unique to Light Craft. I think I was being overly self-critical in blaming myself for the problems when these are the natural occurrences when teams grow. Now that icube™ has given me a clear process and method to tackle these issues, I feel much more energized and enthusiastic about my work. My team is so much happier. Can I say that? They aren't working any less or any harder, but they are so much more fulfilled!"

"Ding, ding, ding! The insight of the year award goes to Diana Becker!" Robert proclaimed. "Diana, I was hoping to see the day when I would hear you say that. From the first day we discussed icube™, I had no doubt in your abilities and leadership. All you needed was the system and method. I am looking forward to watching Light Craft grow into an international player in the lighting business."

"Now I have a favor to ask you, Diana," he continued. "I was waiting until you got back from GOLD before bringing this up. A2Z is experiencing a growth spurt, and we've been approached by a strategic partner. They want to buy a piece of the business and make a financial investment in the company. It will mean a nice chunk of change for Julie and me, but more important, it will give A2Z the resources for some next level of growth that I've been contemplating for a while. It will require focus and some strategizing to get there. Our partner wants to establish a board, and they will have some representation on it. They also want me to nominate two directors to the board. I have one in mind who has tentatively accepted. I was hoping you would accept the other position."

"Wow! That's quite an honor, Robert. Are you sure I would be able to carry out the responsibilities?"

"Without a doubt, Diana! I have absolutely no hesitation. A mind like yours could really help us out. I don't think you see it as much as I do, but you have a unique set of skills and perspective that I don't see in many people. Also, now that you have icube™, I think you have the bandwidth and an understanding of how we work as a team. So, what do you think?"

"Holy cow, Robert! This is not at all what I had expected. Well, I wouldn't be in the position I'm in if it weren't for your guidance and introducing me to icube™. Absolutely! I'm in."

As they walked to their cars, Robert entered a reminder in his phone to send Diana the A2Z board member onboarding package. Diana walked to her car with a big grin. With that, and with best wishes to Diana, Robert, and their companies, now let's turn for the last time to you to do the final check-in of this book.

Vision Track

- ◇ How are you feeling right now?
- ◇ Can you visualize the changes that could occur in your organization if you facilitated icube™?

Action Track To-Dos

◇ Is your company ready for departmental tactical meetings?

◇ Learn about gainsharing and see how this applies to your business. Are there already elements in the scorecard that you could use for this purpose?

◇ Is your company ready for a board? Can you list the types of people you would want as directors?

◇ Perform an audit of all your information systems. Are they supporting the flow of information necessary to execute the mission and vision of your company?

I hope you have found this book as inspirational and motivating as it has been for me to write it. I look forward to hearing your story as you take your company on the icube™ journey. Please send a note to learnmore@pcsinsight.com when you have a moment. Thank you.

Appendix: Robert and Meetings

Note to reader: The following is based on true events. The names have been changed to protect the embarrassed.

Robert started A2Z Distributing in the late 70s, focusing on the Metro Detroit area as an aftermarket supplier of specialized automotive components. With blood, sweat, and tears, he built a successful company that dominated the niche market. A2Z's focus on excellent service made it a no brainer for customers to do business with them. Manufacturers took notice and offered A2Z a coveted master distributor status with attractive credit terms. Robert took the opportunity and built a brand that became well known within its circles. Along the way, he also made a couple of key hires, Mark and Dave, as his "lieutenants." Mark was in charge of sales and operations, while Dave was in charge of purchasing, both critical functions for a distribution company.

Over the years, Robert, ever the visionary, set the directive for the company and expected Mark and Dave to execute his vision. Mark, while extremely intelligent, was not exactly a people person. An expert of the industry, he single-handedly made decisions related to process, delivery, customers, and pricing. He had no need for anyone's input, and to his credit, he was often correct in his judgements. Dave, on the other hand, was the consummate schmoozer. Even though he wasn't heading sales, he was an industry insider who most customers knew and respected. They always took his calls, and he made sure to build a relationship with all the key people and business owners. He seemed to have a "spider" sense for what they wanted. As the purchaser, he got the inside scoop from supplier representatives and used that to negotiate the best possible pricing and terms for A2Z.

In essence, Mark loved process; Dave loved people. While Mark was a whiz with the company's software system and had knack for efficiency, Dave only knew how to create purchase orders. Over time, these two leaders drifted apart and the company operated with an atmosphere of uneasy détente. Some long-term employees like Donna, the on-road sales person, respected Mark but found it easier to talk to Dave. Phil, the warehouse manager, liked Mark's discipline but coordinated inventory purchases with Dave. Robert, not necessarily a numbers guy, asked Alice, the controller, to develop the general ledger chart of accounts and the accounting system, which he didn't fully understand himself. Mark and Dave, who needed this information, often felt that Alice was hiding information under Robert's direction, but they wouldn't come out and say it.

So, while the going was good, A2Z thrived in spite of itself. The market needed the product, and if there was one thing they did well, it was to deliver product. On the outside, this company looked like it was successful, and it was. However, over the years, it had also missed some great opportunities, and Robert who had a nose for business sensed that something was wrong. And the latest issue brought all of this to a head.

It turned out that A2Z's biggest supplier, Danco Industrial, which was owned by a private equity investment group, was going through a crisis. The owners had distributed too much cash out of the company and its manufacturing output had taken a hit. When Danco's suppliers tightened credit, A2Z started experiencing backorders on the Danco products that flowed right to their customers.

Initially, the customers were understanding, and things went on with promises such as, "We are just around the corner on this," from Danco's representative. Around the same time, Dave over estimated inventory purchases from another vendor, Lightsteel Fabrication, and with the reduced cash flow from all the backorders, A2Z was past due with Lightsteel. To make matters worse, a newcomer, Orient Metalz, entered the market and executed a marketing campaign targeting A2Z's customers with a product line overlapping Danco's and Lightsteel's lines. Orient Metalz was an importer and had a substantial cost advantage over Danco and Lightsteel who manufactured locally. Their quality, however, was hit or miss.

Customers loyal to the two incumbents had kept Orient from getting a foothold in the market. However, Orient saw Danco's weakness as the opportunity it was looking for and sprang into action. By going directly to A2Z's customers with promises of lower pricing, it started getting attention. A2Z's customers were losing sales on the Danco product line and many argued that it would be better to sell something than nothing. Orient still needed a distributor and approached A2Z with an attractive pricing and terms. However, the offer came with conditions. A2Z needed to carry the entire product line, thus replacing Danco and Lightsteel in one fell swoop. If A2Z refused, Orient would go to its biggest competitor, JK Brothers, a much smaller company but one that was always looking for an opportunity to undermine A2Z. The repercussions of such a move would not be trivial. On the one hand, Danco was struggling but not dead. Their shortage could very well be temporary. And A2Z owed money to Lightsteel. If it agreed to do business with Orient, it would be jeopardizing a relationship that had been built over years with two of its biggest vendors. On the other hand, saying no to Orient would mean giving JK an advantage in the marketplace. Loyalty to Danco and Lightsteel could turn out to be quite costly. Robert knew in his gut that he couldn't make this decision lightly. He needed the insight and brainpower of his entire team to set the direction. At this point, Robert turned to icube™ facilitator, Pam Schaffer, for help.

"Do we *have* to?!" whined Robert to Pam when they finally got together. She looked up in astonishment. His usual confidence and split-second, surefooted decision-making demeanor was gone. All she had done was suggest he have a meeting with his leadership team to discuss an important strategic decision. "You know what?" he added. "Most meetings suck, and unless you convince me otherwise, I'm not doing this!" With that, he crossed his arms and leaned back in his chair.

Pam knew he didn't much care for meetings, but she didn't know she'd get such a strong allergic reaction. But Robert didn't have all the information he needed to make an important decision, and he knew it. He could wing it, but he'd be putting the company at great risk. Pam knew they had to resolve Robert's meeting aversion before they could move forward, so she suggested that, just for the heck of it, they brainstorm why most meetings suck! Here's the list they came up with:

1. Unclear goals
2. Unclear agenda
3. Unclear who's running the meeting

4. Unclear what is expected of each individual, including participation level

5. Uneven participation from all attendees

6. Lack of follow-through and accountability

7. Poor time management

8. Technology distractions

After they reviewed this list, she shared the icube™ general meeting agenda with Robert. He looked it over and after he was convinced that it addressed all the issues that were identified, he sent his team the following email:

You don't see a lot of emails from me calling for a team meeting. In fact, you probably know that I hate them. However, the company is faced with a critical decision right now, and the matter is serious enough that we need to gather all the facts and ensure that we do this as a team. Hence, I am calling for a meeting with the five of us. Details are below:
    When: Friday at 9:00 am
    Where: Conference Room
    How long: 90 minutes
    Meeting Leader: Robert
    Attendees: Alice, Mark, Dave, and Donna
Special Note: My promise is that this meeting won't go over 90 minutes. We need your full attention; therefore, I ask that you leave your cellphones and laptops behind.

Agenda

Goals

- Clarity and agreement on Danco situation

- Clarity and agreement on Lightsteel relationship

- Clarity and agreement on next steps for how to respond to Orient's offer

Topics

- Situation overview: Robert
- Financial review: Alice
  - Projected performance if we stay with Danco and Lightsteel
  - Projected performance if we switch to Orient
- Danco update: Mark and Dave
- Lightsteel past due and payment update: Alice and Dave
- Orient market perception: Donna and Dave
- JK Brothers market perception: Donna
- Key questions to answer: All
  - Will Danco make it?
  - Will the JK/Orient match up prove to be a serious threat?
  - What is the upside and downside of each decision?
  - Is there any other option for us to pursue?

Issues

We will list issues on the white board as they come up so we don't get sidetracked.

To-Dos

We will capture to-dos for follow-up and our next meeting.

I know this is different from the way we have done things before, so please let me know if you have any questions, and be prepared to update the team on the topic if your name is next to it.
Thanks!
Robert

The following Friday the team met for the first time in years. It was a bit rough in the beginning, but they followed the agenda. Alice, Donna, and Mark had "to-dos" that Robert captured during the meeting. The team met again the following Friday, and Robert used the same agenda outline with different topics, starting with a review of the previous week's "to-dos." Alice and Mark had theirs done but Donna had not. But she caught on pretty quickly that she was accountable for getting them done. The A2Z leadership team continued meeting this way for a few more weeks until they had all the information and intel needed to make their decision. They decided to stick with Danco and Lightsteel and politely decline Orient's offer.

Orient signed on JK as a distributor, but after Danco's manufacturing issues were resolved, the partnership fizzled. Donna reported scuttlebutt that JK was into Orient for over $1.5M dollars and wasn't keeping up on payments. In the meantime, Mark and the rest of the team asked Robert if they could continue to have the team meetings every Friday. They also asked Robert to lead the team meetings. Since the change in their meeting process had been so successful, Robert ended up taking the company through the whole icube™ process. They are still practicing it today. The last Pam heard, A2Z had grown an average of eighteen percent each year since implementing icube™.

References

"About Us." Retrieved May 13, 2016 from https://www.oxfam.org/en/our-purpose-and-beliefs.

Bae, H., April 6, 2015. *Bill Gates' 40th Anniversary email: Goal was 'A Computer on Every Desk.'* Retrieved May 13, 2016 from http://money.cnn.com/2015/04/05/technology/bill-gates-email-microsoft-40-anniversary/

Carpenter, J., May 31, 2016, *Boston Beer Company's Jim Koch on the Crucial Different between Dangerous and Merely Scary.* Retrieved December 21, 2016 from http://www.forbes.com/sites/johncarpenter1/2016/05/31/boston-beer-companys-jim-koch-on-the-crucial-difference-between-dangerous-and-merely-scary/

Kirkland, R., November, 2013, *Leading in the 21st Century: An Interview with Ford's Alan Mulally.* Retrieved January 2016 from http://www.mckinsey.com/business-functions/strategy-and-corporate-finance/our-insights/leading-in-the-21st-century-an-interview-with-fords-alan-mulally

Luft & Ingham, 1955. "The Johari window [is] a graphic model of interpersonal awareness." Proceedings of the western training laboratory in group development (Los Angeles: University of California, Los Angeles).

Signore, D., *Second Stage Sensei*, Retrieved September 15, 2016 from http://edwardlowe.org/second-stage-sensei/

www.ingramcontent.com/pod-product-compliance
Lightning Source LLC
LaVergne TN
LVHW081524060526
838200LV00044B/1991